Learning Disabilities
DIAGNOSTIC-PRESCRIPTIVE INSTRUMENTS

Learning Disabilities
DIAGNOSTIC-PRESCRIPTIVE INSTRUMENTS

Robert E. Valett, Ed.D.
Professor of Education
California State University, Fresno,
and Consulting Psychologist

Lear Siegler, Inc./Fearon Publishers
Belmont, California

Copyright © 1973 by Lear Siegler, Inc.,/Fearon Publishers, 6 Davis Drive, Belmont, California 94002. All rights reserved. No part of this book may be reproduced by any means, nor transmitted, nor translated into a machine language, without written permission from Fearon Publishers.

ISBN-0-8224-4255-8
Library of Congress Catalog Card Number: 72-93426
Printed in the United States of America.

LC
4704
.V35

This book is dedicated to the memory of Jean Itard (1774-1838), the father of developmental task analysis and prescriptive teaching.

CONTENTS

PART 1   Rationale 1

    1 The Diagnostic-prescriptive Process / 3
    2 The Psychoeducational Evaluation of Human Behavior / 7
    3 The Psychoeducational Report / 12

PART 2   Instruments for Psychoeducational Evaluation 17

    4 A Basic Screening and Referral Form for Children with Suspected Learning and Behavioral Difficulties / 19
    5 Developmental Task Analysis / 31
    6 An Inventory of Primary Skills / 37
    7 A Psychoeducational Inventory of Basic Learning Abilities / 53
    8 Self-evaluation Devices / 87
    9 Specifying Priority Objectives / 92

PART 3   Case Studies and Applications 101

    10 Using Task Analysis with Intelligence Testing: Jay / 103
    11 Using the Psychoeducational Inventory and the Developmental Task Analysis: Mitch / 114
    12 Applying Diagnostic Findings to Prescriptive Suggestions: Robbie / 124
    13 Behavior Records and the Specification of Objectives: T. W. / 133
    14 Task Analysis and the Development of Social Behavior: Peri / 142
    15 The Learning Resource Center Model / 147
    16 Using the Learning Resource Center: Beverly / 153
    17 The Evaluation and Development of Basic Learning Abilities: Billy J. / 161

    Index / 173

FIGURES

Figure 1   The Diagnostic-Prescriptive Process / 4
Figure 2   The Psychoeducational Evaluation of Human Behavior / 8
Figure 3   A Model Outline for a Psychoeducational Report / 13
Figure 4   A Psychoeducational Evaluation of Basic Learning Abilities / 56
Figure 5   Basic Learning Abilities Inventory Summary and Prescriptive Implications / 57
Figure 6   Recommended Psychoeducational Programs and Materials / 58
Figure 7   Perceptual Motor Skills (Part I) / 59
Figure 8   A School Profile of Basic Learning Abilities for Twenty Pupils / 60
Figure 9   A Self-Evaluation Check Sheet / 88
Figure 10   My Goal Record / 91
Figure 11   Determining Individual Learning Objectives / 93
Figure 12   Specific Behavior Record / 96
Figure 13   Self-Report of Daily Learning Objectives / 98
Figure 14   Baseline Data: T.W. / 135
Figure 15   Baseline and Treatment Data: T.W. / 138
Figure 16   Learning Resource Center for Exceptional Children: Educational Therapy Plan / 156

PREFACE

An instrument is a tool for accomplishing a given purpose. A diagnostic-prescriptive instrument provides a means for understanding a pupil by determining some of his learning strengths and weaknesses and their behavioral implications. If we are to become involved in actually teaching a child, these instruments should help us in deciding what we should teach and what priorities we should assign to the varied learning tasks. This is the first and most important job of the diagnostic-prescriptive teacher, since without careful pupil evaluation and subsequent specification of learning objectives, the resulting educational program may be grossly inadequate, even deleterious to the child's welfare.

This book is written for those interested in the diagnostic-prescriptive teaching of exceptional children. Its emphasis is on the evaluation and prescriptive programming of children with significant learning and behavioral problems. Although students of learning disabilities, special educators, prescriptive specialists, and school psychologists will find the material of immediate relevance, general classroom teachers and others concerned with individualized instruction may also find it of value.

I have attempted to bring together here a number of the instruments that I have devised over the years for use by diagnostic-prescriptive teachers. All of these instruments are practical tools that teachers can use to help them arrive at realistic goals and expectations for working with learning-disabled children and their parents. None of the instruments presented is a standardized test with normative statistics for given population groups. Instead, they are what I prefer to term "criterion instruments"; they include a number of important and varied curricular tasks and expectations with which parents and teachers have long been concerned. Some of the instruments are systematic approaches and guides for determining and recording behavioral objectives and their achievement. The major purpose is to provide varied means whereby the teacher may survey critical learning tasks (1) to aid in determining specific educational objectives and (2) to select possible disability areas that may require further study or referral to consulting specialists such as psychologists and physicians.

It has been my position that special educators are most effective when they begin their work with the direct behavioral observation and personal assessment of those children assigned to them. This approach requires immediate involvement in the "psychoeducational process" and demands that the teacher look at the child's behavior as a function of the educational setting. The evaluation procedures essential to this process require consideration of specific developmental tasks and their degree of accomplishment. Instruments used in this process should enable the teacher to gain a broader perspective of the child, and thereby contribute to the many value judgments she must make as to what the child should be taught.

The rationale and instruments presented in this book are formative and incomplete by themselves. They will undoubtedly be revised and extended in the years to come. It is also acknowledged that the book is inadequate by itself as a comprehensive text in prescriptive procedures. However, the intent is to indicate how prescriptive implications and procedures can be derived from such instruments as these, and this kind of application is illustrated by the case studies presented in Part III. Those readers whose main concern is with the prescriptive use of developmental or remedial education and techniques are referred to my other publications for supplemental readings and programs in this area. Many other instruments are also available for diagnostic-prescriptive teaching, and no attempt has been made to include them here; readers new to the field should consult other standard texts on the diagnosis and remediation of learning disabilities before deciding what their own approach should be.

I must extend my thanks to the many fine diagnostic-prescriptive teachers and psychologists with whom I have been privileged to work through the years. Special thanks are due to those former students of mine who contributed case studies, and they are specifically acknowledged in Part III; my debt to them is great, for I have learned from them as I hope they have learned from me. I also wish to thank *Exceptional Children* and *Journal of School Psychology* for permission to reprint the articles that appear here as Chapters 15 and 17, respectively.

I hope that readers will find these instruments of value and be able to adapt them to their own needs. I will welcome suggestions for modification or extension of the materials, and I would be especially grateful if those conducting studies on specific applicability of any of these instruments would kindly send me a copy of their findings.

Robert E. Valett

PART 1

RATIONALE

The first part of this book introduces the reader to the rationale underlying the use of diagnostic-prescriptive instruments. Chapter 1 presents a nine-step diagnostic-prescriptive process as a basis for educational planning and for the programming of children with learning difficulties. Chapter 2 outlines a model for the psychoeducational evaluation of human behavior that emphasizes the critical factors to be evaluated. In Chapter 3, the components of the psychoeducational report are briefly discussed as a guide to prescriptive teaching, and the importance of deriving specific recommendations from assessment data is stressed. Throughout Part 1, the teacher is recognized as the key person in the diagnostic-prescriptive process.

CHAPTER 1
The diagnostic-prescriptive process

The diagnostic-prescriptive process is composed of nine steps (see Figure 1). The first step in the process occurs when the classroom teacher begins to formulate an hypothesis of a possible learning problem. This usually happens when one of her students continues to experience difficulty in meeting her expectations. The "problem behavior" itself may be in the academics, such as reading; or it may be in psychomotor areas, as evidenced in arts or games. Many problem behaviors also appear in the affective realm of interpersonal relations and self-control; these may result in classroom disturbance that prompts the teacher to hypothesize that something must be wrong with the child. Initial hypotheses usually have two major educational implications. The first is that if something is found to be "wrong" with the child, perhaps he can be removed from the class for special education (possibly assigned to another classroom!). Therefore, the hypothesis tends to be formulated in terms of possible mental retardation, emotional disturbance, neurological involvement, or other disabilities as a reasonable basis for referral. The second implication of the initial hypotheses is, "There may be some way that *I* can be more effective in helping this child to learn—if only I had someone to help me!" The implication here is that something may be "wrong" with the teaching-instructional program and curricular expectations, and that it may be instrumental in producing the observed problem behavior. In any case, once the teacher has reached the point of speculation, she is usually ready to initiate the second step of screening and referral.

It is here that the diagnostic-prescriptive process usually breaks down, for few school districts provide the means whereby teachers can become involved in the early screening and identification of learning problems. A simple one-page referral form is usually grossly inadequate. What is required is some detailed screening procedure that will enable the teacher to specify and describe those behaviors of concern to her. *A Basic Screening and Referral Form for Children with Suspected Learning and Behavioral Disabilities* (see pages 19–29) is one means of providing this description. Another is for the teacher to provide behavioral samples from task assignments; these are usually work samples that the child has produced, but they may also include anecdotal records, unit tests, etc.

At this point, the pupil himself should be brought into the process. Most individuals, including very young children, have some degree of self-awareness, including certain self-concepts that can be conveyed to those they feel are genuinely concerned about them. It is essential that the learner himself become involved as early as possible in the diagnostic-prescriptive process if insight and motivation

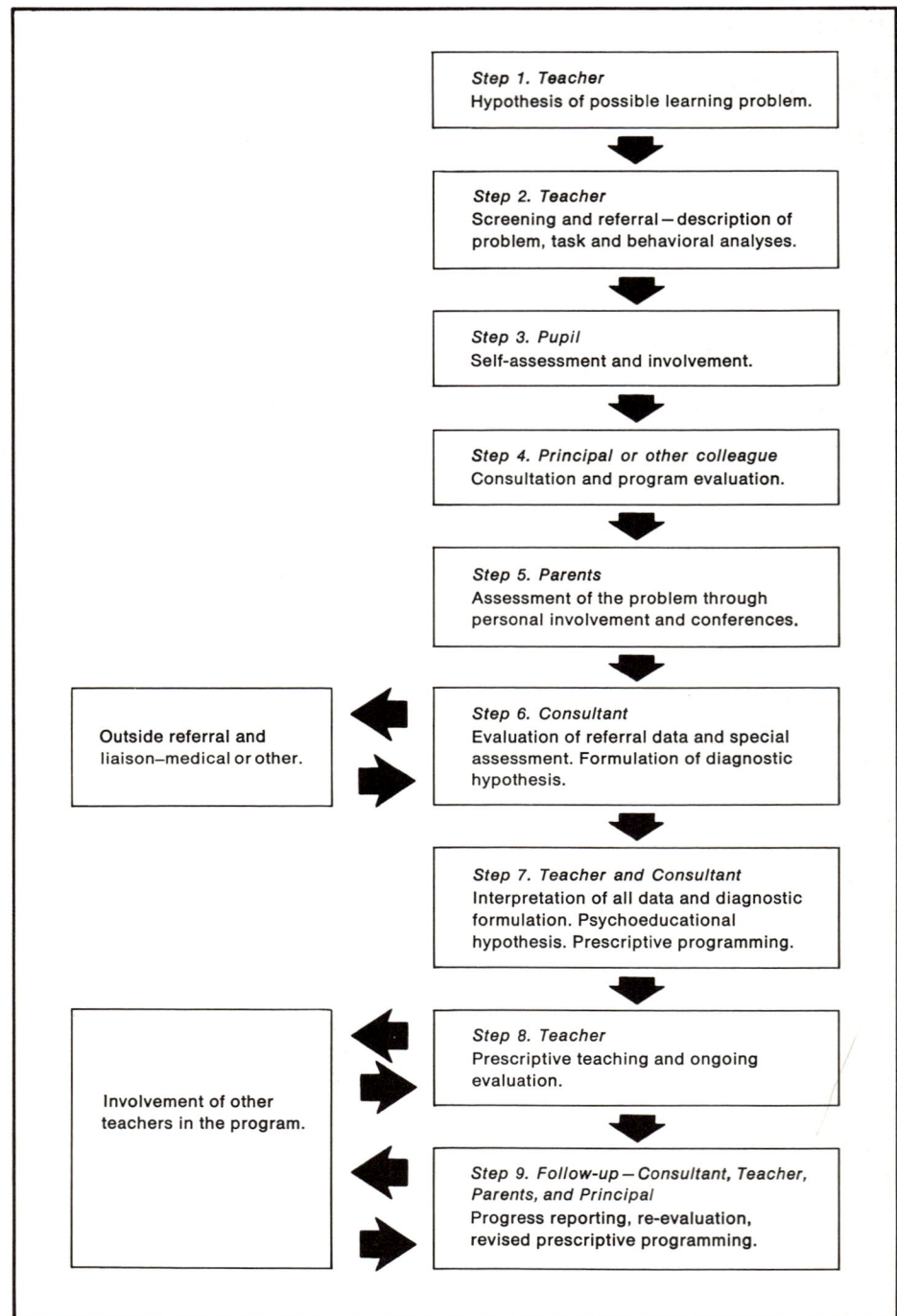

Figure 1. The diagnostic-prescriptive process

are to be fruitfully developed. This involvement can be developed by talking with the pupil about the problem behavior as perceived by others and obtaining his own view of the problem. Once mutual discussion of the problem has begun, the child can begin to assess his own strengths and weaknesses and help to propose alternative actions and reasonable self-expectancies. The means for pupil self-assessment are many and varied; they include everything from self-rating checklists and tests to simple self-report sheets such as those in Chapter 8. Whatever the means, the basic assumption is that the learner himself must be immediately involved in the consideration of his own behavior.

Following pupil self-assessment, there should be the involvement in the process of a third party. This is usually done quite informally through after-school discussion of the "learning problem" with a respected colleague or the school principal. In most cases, the colleague is a fellow teacher who has had a similar experience and can bring a different perspective to the problem. Through review of the screening data and work samples and informal discussion of the program expectancies, other valid alternatives are usually recognized. Some schools have formalized this process by establishing a school guidance committee of five or six experienced teachers whose job it is to meet weekly for consultations with their colleagues about learning problems and possible referrals to outside sources. In a great number of cases, this consultation proves sufficient in dealing with the problem.

Before any referral is made to a consultant outside the regular classroom, the parents should be involved in the assessment of the problem through their own evaluation of their child and through conferences with the referring teacher. All parents have considerable information about the learning assets and limitations, successes and failures, and interests of their children. If requested, they can provide much help to the school in understanding the problem, in further assessment by means of their own systematic observation or checklists, and even in proposals respecting the learning objectives to be given priority. Where cooperative involvement of parents is planned for and instituted at an early stage, the pupil benefits immeasurably and much future misunderstanding may be prevented.

The consultant appears at the sixth step in the diagnostic-prescriptive process. In most cases, this consultant is a school psychologist or an educational specialist, such as a learning-disability diagnostic-prescriptive teacher, who serves one or more schools. In larger schools or in schools with special programs, it is often possible (and highly desirable) to have a diagnostic-prescriptive teacher assigned full time to one school; in these cases, the consultant works out of a resource room that children and regular classroom teachers visit whenever it is necessary and desirable. The first responsibility of the consultant is to collate and evaluate all of the screening and referral data on hand. The next responsibility includes special supplemental assessment of the pupil (which usually requires direct classroom observation), further specific task analysis of the referred behavior, and testing as necessary. Further referral to medical or community agencies may be made at this point. The process then requires the consultant to formulate an extended diagnostic hypothesis for joint follow-up with the referring teacher.

The seventh step in the diagnostic-prescriptive process is by far the most important one, for it is here that the referring teacher and the consultant *jointly* review and consider all data and their educational implications. It is essential that this be done through one or more personal conferences so that a working psychoeducational hypothesis will be formulated cooperatively as the basis for prescriptive programming. The prescriptive program itself is predicated on the assumption that the child can first be helped in his present learning situation through the development of an individualized continuous-progress program relevant to his needs. To develop such a supplemental program, the teacher needs supportive help, which may include new learning materials, redesign of the learning environment, prescriptive consultation, individual educational therapy or tutoring, and community services. In a few cases, the required prescriptive program may necessitate moving the child to a classroom where very special equipment, intensive instruction, and trained aides are provided.

The teacher then proceeds to implement the prescriptive program. In most cases, this is the responsibility of the regular classroom teacher, who is assigned a number of pupils for varied instructional purposes. The severely handicapped child, such as the profoundly deaf or the trainable mentally retarded, may require a specially assigned teacher. However, prescriptive teaching requires that *all* teachers having contact with the pupil be aware of his needs and be involved in meeting them. Therefore, it is essential to the furthering of the prescriptive process and the ongoing evaluation that the teacher who is assigned the child also serve as liaison with other teachers in the school.

The success of any diagnostic-prescriptive program depends on the extent to which follow-up services are provided for the pupil and his classroom teacher. It is obvious, for example, that the consultant must have frequent contact with the pupil to ensure that his learning problem and needs are being sufficiently met by the new prescriptive program. It is less obvious, but of equal importance, that the consultant involve other teachers in understanding and directly helping the child with significant prescriptive needs. The consultant should also maintain contact with the child's parents and the school principal and help to design a pupil-progress reporting and re-evaluation system whereby the child can be aided and encouraged to continue his learning. The final step of follow-up also recognizes that the learning objective is seldom fully realized, and that ongoing revision of the prescriptive program is both necessary and desirable. Although minor revision of the prescriptive program is inherently continuous, major revisions requiring additional consultant time may need to be considered once or twice a year (usually in January and in June).

This model of the diagnostic-prescriptive process emphasizes the critical importance of the teacher. The referring teacher, the regular classroom teacher receiving the learning-disabled child, and the diagnostic-prescriptive teacher-consultant all possess the required skills and potentialities whereby the child with significant learning problems can be aided to learn more effectively. Specific techniques, instruments, and case illustrations of the diagnostic-prescriptive process comprise the remainder of this book.

CHAPTER 2
The psychoeducational evaluation of human behavior

The diagnostic-prescriptive teacher-consultant is constantly involved in the psychoeducational evaluation and programming of human behavior. Psychoeducational evaluation refers to the assessment of a child's behavior in a given educational setting. Psychoeducational evaluation assumes that the learner's behavior is the result of his personal interaction with his environment. Therefore, the assessment procedure must include evaluation of the individual's receptive perceptual-motor channels (R_c), his mediational processes (M_p), and his expressive modalities (E_m). These factors must then be considered relative to the specific environmental determinants in which the person finds himself (e). His behavioral response (B) can then be expressed by the following formula:

$$B = f(e) \cdot (R_c + M_p + E_m)$$

which reads that behavior is a function (f) of the integrity of individual receptive perceptual-motor channels plus mediational processes and the expressive modalities as they interact with the environment. The evaluation and analysis of specific behavior (B) is an essential prerequisite for the determination of priority educational objectives and the design of any subsequent learning program. The component parts of the psychoeducational evaluation are presented in Figure 2, and need to be considered in some detail.

RECEPTIVE PERCEPTUAL-MOTOR CHANNELS

Perceptual-motor channels are those basic sensory processes by which the learner receives and acquires information or skills from his environment. The essential question for the consultant to answer is: Are sensory stimuli (information, etc.) actually getting into the learner? There are many central and peripheral problems of the brain and its nervous system, such as deafness, visual limitations, and varied convulsive anomalies, that have obvious educational implications. Inasmuch as many children with learning disabilities suffer from minimal brain dysfunction or slight sensory impairments, some attempt should always be made to appraise the integrity of the receptive channels. This appraisal is usually done through a gross observation by the consultant, who must then determine whether medical or other referral may be needed for more specific diagnosis and treatment.

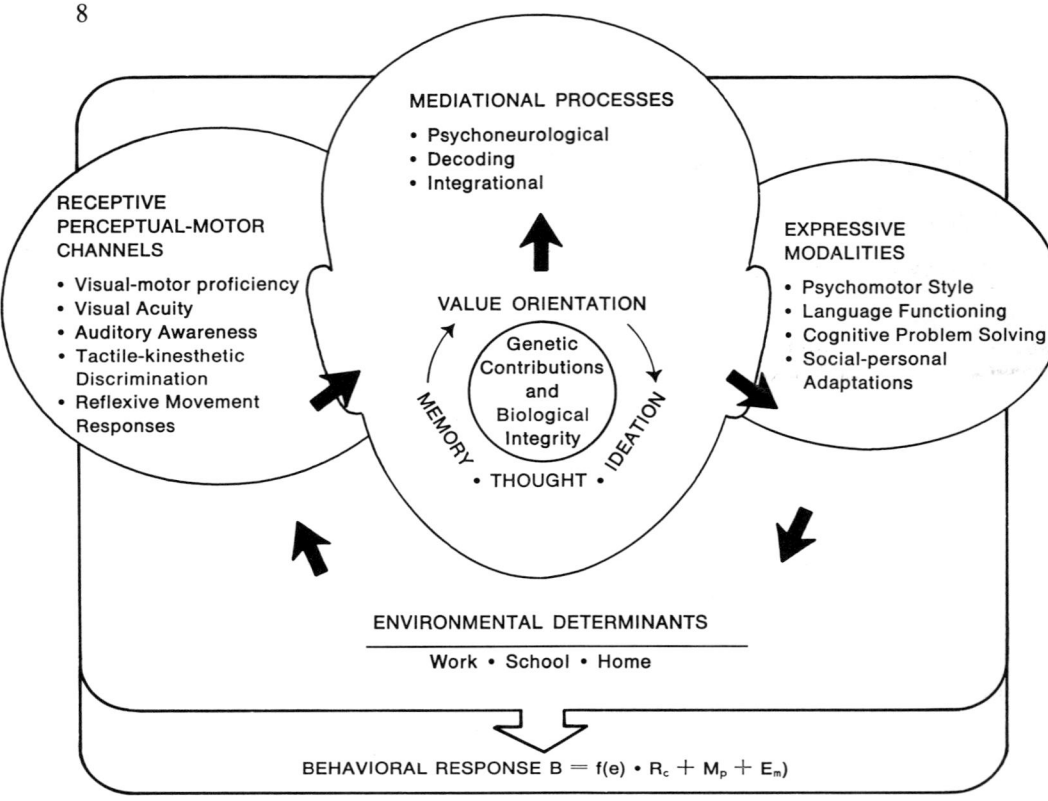

Figure 2. The psychoeducational evaluation of human behavior

The receptive channels requiring teacher evaluation are those that are of immediate importance in any learning program. Are the child's basic reflexive movement responses adequate to the extent that he has motor control required in play, games, and numerous physical learning activities? Can he make fundamental tactile-kinesthetic discriminations with his hands and skin, such as naming and differentiating hidden objects and responding adequately to pain, pressure, and other direct forms of physical stimulation? Is his auditory awareness intact to the extent that he can attend, listen, and respond to directions? Does he have the visual acuity required to see, coordinate, and integrate his learning experiences, or are visual anomalies suspected? Has he demonstrated visual motor proficiency to the extent that he is able to use his eyes, hands, and body in an integrated and coordinated manner within the learning situation?

The teacher may use many methods in her evaluation of these basic receptive perceptual-motor channels. Certainly, one of the best is her careful observation and noting of the individual's responses to the demands of the educational program. Any unusual response can be recorded in an anecdotal record. A number of screening or behavior-rating forms can be helpful in pointing out those important behaviors to be observed. Inventories and specific task-analysis procedures presented in this book can also be used for this purpose.

MEDIATIONAL PROCESSES

The mediational processes are those that decode or interpret the incoming receptive sensory data and then determine what meaning and importance should be attached to them. These processes are largely psychoneurological in that they are rooted in the genetic qualities and biology of the organism. For instance, a chromosomal abnormality may result in limited perceptual functioning, may interfere with general memory and comprehension abilities, or may even interfere with thought and ideation. In a similar fashion, system defects within the brain itself may make it difficult or impossible for the person to integrate his sensory experiences in a functional way. The diagnostic-prescriptive teacher, however, must be primarily concerned with the nature or qualities of the personal value orientations and the memory, thought, and associative processes of the learner. What is of crucial importance here is the determination of what his experiences "mean" to the learner and how he feels about his memories, thoughts, and associations.

For example, auditory-visual memory and the ability to sequence learned experiences are essential components of functional human behavior; the child with specific difficulty in these abilities usually experiences trouble in reading and problem solving. For a similar example, the unique thoughts and ideas resulting from human experience are interrelated and associated with one another in such a way that a distinctive approach to learning results. This individual approach gradually becomes a "learning style" that reflects thinking processes and affective-emotive characteristics. The "value" that the learner gives to his thoughts and experiences results from the developing life interests, need satisfactions, and subjective feelings that gradually crystallize into an attitude toward further learning. These personal value orientations then act as a sieve through which incoming sensory data are processed to determine in what way, and to what extent, the individual should invest his energy in varied expressive forms.

The diagnostic-prescriptive teacher can evaluate these mediational processes in part by observing and noting how the learner spends his time—what he invests his energy in or what he gives himself to. His use of free time in school and at home—his hobbies, clubs, reading interests and other extracurricular activities—all reflect his value orientations. Informal conversations with the child are often enlightening. Direct questioning and the use of value inventories, autobiographies, incomplete sentences, creative stories, and various tests also provide insight into understanding how the child thinks, what he feels, and why he may act or respond as he does.

EXPRESSIVE MODALITIES

There are numerous ways, or modes, of expressing human behavior. However the individual expresses himself, he tends to use several major modalities at once, although one may be emphasized. Thus, if we observe eleven-year-old Billy playing basketball, we can detect that body movement is his major means of immediate problem solving, although we can also see that language and interpersonal adaptations are also being expressed as he moves about the court.

Psychomotor style is perhaps the basic expressive modality. It is a body language that includes posture, gait, movement, and gesture; and it reflects both sensory-motor integration and personal value orientation. The person who is anxious, tense, or fearful often reflects these affective states in his psychomotor behavior. Language functioning is expressed in the way the person speaks, reads, and writes, and also in the symbolic languages of art, music, and mathematics—all of which convey experience and meaning. The child also expresses himself through specific cognitive styles or approaches to problem solving. One child, for instance, may be precise, analytical, and convergent in his thinking and approach to problems, whereas another may be synthetic, divergent, or evaluative. Although widely varied forms of human expression should be recognized and valued in their own right, it is important for the learner to develop minimal proficiency in the basic skills of language and of cognitive problem solving so that he may have the flexibility of choice demanded in modern life.

All human skills and abilities are brought to bear on problems of social and personal adaptation. Accordingly, it is impossible to evaluate social-personal adaptation apart from language and other expressive modalities. But there are distinctive forms of personal adaptation to self and environment that require careful evaluation. The way or manner in which the child relates to his peers has many educational implications. Some of the specific behaviors that are important to note and evaluate here are tendencies toward involvement and participation, friendliness, and social responsibility, versus isolation-withdrawal, shyness, aggressiveness, and noncooperation. The child's repertoire of social skills, including such things as knowledge of peer-group interests and games and the use of jokes and humor, should be noted. On the secondary school level, all other skills and abilities culminate in a social style and in personal-identity behaviors that should be given priority in the evaluation process.

In addition to direct behavioral assessment, there are many instruments available for use in assessing the expressive modalities. These include, among others: physical education skill tests, standardized reading tests, psycholinguistic achievement batteries, abstract tests of basic skills and problem solving, social-personal inventories, and on-the-job life-performance evaluations. The *Psychoeducational Inventory of Basic Learning Abilities* (see pages 61–86) is a task-analytic instrument that presents numerous samples of learning tasks in all of these modalities. It is frequently used as an initial means of evaluating expressive behaviors.

ENVIRONMENTAL DETERMINANTS

The psychoeducational evaluation is incomplete if it excludes the environment in which the learner is living. We now know that the particular structure of the environment itself is a significant determinant of human behavior. The pressure and demands of the home, of the school program, and of the work situation have powerful rewards and consequences that directly shape the behavior of the child. It is, therefore, fallacious to assume that assessing the learner himself is all that is necessary in order to develop a meaningful educational program. It is wiser to assume that much of the child's behavior is a response to the unique demands of the programs, materials, and people with which he is constantly involved.

The importance of environment is most apparent when we evaluate the physical facilities of certain homes, schools, or work centers; insufficient food, clothing, furniture, lighting, materials, and equipment greatly influence the child's mode of behavior. Within the school, grouping, the method of school organization, and class placement and grading policies have obvious repercussions. Similarly, the classroom environment, especially the nature of the daily schedule, the learning materials available, and the teacher's expectations (realistic or unrealistic), greatly influences and modifies the child's behavior. The diagnostic-prescriptive teacher must not only be aware of these determinants, but must also make some systematic attempt to assess the degree to which they are producing desirable or undesirable behaviors. Special attention must be given to determining parental and teacher expectancies, opportunities for meeting them, and the consequences involved for the learner.

SUMMARY

A model for the psychoeducational evaluation of human behavior has been presented. The focus in this model is on the diagnostic-prescriptive teacher, whose primary concern is to assess the functional skills and abilities of the learner in order to determine his needs and establish his priority learning objectives. A concomitant purpose is to begin constructing a prescriptive learning program whereby these distinctive needs and objectives may be realized. The evaluation procedure requires assessment of the learner's receptive perceptual-motor channels, of his mediational processes, and of his expressive modalities. It also demands scrutiny of the unique environmental determinants influencing the child, including the specific expectancies of the key people in his life.

CHAPTER 3
The psychoeducational report

The purpose of the psychoeducational report is to inform those persons concerned with the child how he might be helped to learn. Although the report should summarize all available information and evaluation data, it is grossly inadequate if it fails to specify what should be done to aid the child. Psychoeducational reports are usually written by diagnostic-prescriptive teachers, by other educational consultants, or by psychologists. The recipients of such reports are other teachers, allied professionals, and parents. It is common for such reports to be made with a view to initial placement or to eligibility of a child for receiving special developmental or remedial education. Subsequent reports are made approximately once a year and serve as major ongoing re-evaluation summaries for continued educational planning and program revision. A model psychoeducational report outline, which is discussed below, is presented in Figure 3.

PUPIL IDENTIFICATION DATA

The initial part of a psychoeducational report should provide basic identification data, such as the pupil's name, birth date, and chronological age. In addition, the names of the referring teacher and the school and the program or grade level of the child should be clearly indicated.

REASON FOR THE REFERRAL

Every report should contain a brief descriptive statement of the learning or behavior problem and how it is perceived by the referring teacher. Specific teacher concerns should always be reported, since they serve as the basis for the subsequent psychoeducational evaluation. The content of the report itself must then be relevant to these concerns and requests for help. If other reasons for evaluating and working with the child are given as part of the rationale behind the referral, these should also be reported.

INITIAL SCREENING DATA

Although often overlooked in psychoeducational reports, initial screening data invariably provide extremely useful information. Accordingly, it is recommended that four subsections be used for reporting purposes. The first, pertinent history, refers to those obvious health, psychological, and educational factors useful in prescriptive programming. Thus, physical disabilities and special treatment, such as remedial reading or speech therapy, are reported here.

Next comes the data from teacher screening. Referring teachers usually have achievement test results, work samples, anecdotal-baseline data, ratings, and other evaluation information that can be collected and submitted with the referral; it should be summarized here.

Parent screening information should always be included because of the different perspective on the child that it usually provides. Descriptive comments, letters, priority concerns from such instruments as the *Developmental Task Analysis* (see pages 31–36) and from other sources need to be listed briefly.

The child should also be involved in his initial screening, and his self-description and analysis of the referral problem usually comprise a crucial part of the report.

---

1. Pupil Identification Data

2. Reason for the Referral

3. Initial Screening Data
    a. Pertinent history
    b. Teacher screening data
    c. Parent screening data
    d. Pupil self-screening data

4. Evaluation and Test Data Summaries
    a. Social-personal skills and abilities
    b. Conceptual-cognitive skills and abilities
    c. Language skills and abilities
    d. Perceptual skills and abilities
    e. Sensory-motor skills and abilities
    f. Gross motor skills and abilities

5. Performance Interpretations
    a. Specific strengths
    b. Specific weaknesses
    c. Performance style

6. Psychoeducational Implications and Recommendations
    a. Priority learning tasks
    b. Prescriptive programming suggestions
    c. Other comments or recommendations

Figure 3. A model outline for a psychoeducational report

EVALUATION AND TEST DATA SUMMARIES

The fourth section of the report should contain a summary of all evaluation and test data obtained by the diagnostic-prescriptive teacher. It is important, however, that he report these data in a systematic way, not merely list the names of the test and evaluation instruments. It is preferable, therefore, to use a developmental approach that will make it easier for the reader to follow the report and find specific bits of information he may be looking for. The six suggested summary areas are:

> Social-personal skills and abilities
> Conceptual-cognitive skills and abilities
> Language skills and abilities
> Perceptual skills and abilities
> Sensory-motor skills and abilities
> Gross motor skills and abilities.

Under each area, the specific test or instrument used, the date and place administered, the time required, the raw scores, the standard scores, and comparable facts are listed. For example, the *Spache Diagnostic Reading Scale* results would be listed under "Language skills and abilities," the *Wide Range Arithmetic* test results would be listed under "Conceptual-cognitive skills and abilities," and the various parts of the *Psychoeducational Inventory of Basic Learning Abilities* would be reported under the different appropriate subsections. Evaluation and test *summaries* are included on the psychoeducational report so that they may serve as referents for the interpretation and programming sections that follow.

PERFORMANCE INTERPRETATIONS

In the performance interpretations section, the raw evaluation and test data are integrated into a professional judgment that becomes the basis for prescriptive teaching and other interventions deemed necessary. All available data should be interpreted in three subsections of the report. The first concerns the specific strengths of the individual, and should list his outstanding skills and abilities relative to his total performance as well as any special assets, interests, or other attributes he may possess; since most prescriptive teaching usually begins with the strengths of the learner, these must be clearly identified.

Specific weaknesses are then reported—limitations in specific skills or abilities as well as those significant learning or behavioral disabilities that have been identified.

It is also usually wise to report the learner's performance style, which may include general attitude, approach to tasks presented, and unusual responses to items in the tests or parts of the evaluation.

PSYCHOEDUCATIONAL IMPLICATIONS AND RECOMMENDATIONS

The section on psychoeducational implications and recommendations is the most important part of the psychoeducational report. It should contain priority learning tasks, prescriptive programming suggestions, and other comments and recommendations. Unfortunately, this is the part of most reports that proves inadequate. Priority learning tasks should be derived from the entire evaluation and be listed in simple, straightforward language; what the child needs to learn and which top two or three learning tasks are to be emphasized need to be clearly stated if the report is to have any practical value.

Prescriptive programming suggestions for teaching the priority learning tasks should then be presented. Specifying which task the teacher might consider teaching first is always helpful, as are suggested programs, methods, and materials that might be used in teaching these tasks. Most evaluators will make additional comments and recommendations.

END OF THE REPORT

The report should be signed with the name of the evaluator and the date it was completed. The fact that a psychoeducational report has been well prepared may not be a guarantee that it will be used and followed by those reading it, but its acceptance and implementation are much more likely than for a meaningless, jargon-filled, irrelevant report.

PART 2

INSTRUMENTS FOR PSYCHOEDUCATIONAL EVALUATION

A number of criterion instruments for use by diagnostic-prescriptive teachers are presented in this part. All have been devised for initial evaluation purposes, primarily as an aid in selecting teaching objectives. The first instrument presented is *A Basic Screening and Referral Form for Children with Suspected Learning and Behavioral Disabilities,* which is for the use of teachers (Chapter 4). The second instrument, *Developmental Task Analysis,* was devised for parents' use in the evaluation of their own children (Chapter 5). *An Inventory of Primary Skills,* the third instrument, is for use by parents and teachers (Chapter 6). Diagnostic-prescriptive teachers working directly with the child in the development of remedial programs have found the fourth instrument, *A Psychoeducational Inventory of Basic Learning Abilities,* of considerable help (Chapter 7).

Several self-evaluation instruments for use as aids in involving children in the consideration of their personal strengths and weaknesses are presented in Chapter 8. Chapter 9 discusses three means whereby all evaluation data can be integrated to determine priority teaching and learning objectives.

Items reproduced in Part II with the overprinting "Sample" are available as forms from the publisher.

CHAPTER 4

A basic screening and referral form for children with suspected learning and behavioral disabilities

This screening and referral form is to be used by the classroom teacher who is concerned with helping children with suspected learning and behavior disabilities. Its primary purpose is to aid (1) in the early identification of possibly significant learning and behavioral disabilities and (2) in the planning of prescriptive developmental and remedial education. This form should be employed as a basis for collaboration between the teacher and a psycho-educational consultant. It is best used in conjunction with my other diagnostic and remedial materials available from Fearon Publishers.

Pupil's name _____ Birth date _____

Address _____

School _____ Grade/level/program _____

Referring teacher _____ Date referred _____

Copyright, © 1972, by Fearon Publishers/Lear Siegler, Inc., Education Division, 6 Davis Drive, Belmont, California 94002. All rights reserved. No part of this form may be reproduced by any means, nor transmitted, nor translated into a machine language, without written permission from the publisher.

Description of the Problem

A.   Why are you referring this pupil?

B.   Describe the learning or behavior problem in some detail:

C.   How have you attempted to deal with this problem?

D.   If you have discussed this referral with the pupil, describe his reaction and self-perception of the problem:

E.   How do you feel the psychoeducational consultant can best help you at this time?

Pertinent History

A. Comment on the relevant history of this child (health background, medication, special education, therapy):

B. In what has this pupil been most successful in school (subjects, interests, outstanding skills, strengths)?

C. Current performance estimates:
   1. Approximate reading grade placement or level _____
      Comment:

   2. Approximate arithmetic grade placement or level _____
      Comment:

   3. Approximate spelling grade placement or level _____
      Comment:

D. Summary of available achievement tests, ability tests, and diagnostic impressions:

Pupil Behavior Ratings

On pages 4-7 are a number of specific behaviors to be rated as follows:

    0 - This behavior is of no concern at this time.
    1 - This behavior has been exhibited to a noticeable degree and is of some concern to the teacher.
    2 - This behavior has been exhibited to a considerable degree and is of primary concern to the teacher.

After you have marked all behaviors either 0, 1, or 2, quickly review your ratings and place a circle around those behaviors you feel should be given priority consideration. Then write a classroom illustration of these behaviors in the space provided.

Social-personal Behavior Difficulties

Ratings

_____	Easily frustrated	_____	Shy
_____	Uncooperative	_____	Unhappy
_____	Excessive anger	_____	Fearful
_____	Destructive	_____	Anxious
_____	Bizarre	_____	Delusional
_____	Fights frequently	_____	Cruel
_____	Obscene	_____	Disruptive
_____	Profane	_____	Defiant
_____	Lies	_____	Withdrawn
_____	Steals	_____	Tardy
_____	Sullen	_____	Over-conforming

_____ Depressed
_____ Does not accept social responsibility
_____ Difficulty in judging right and wrong
_____ Cannot predict consequences of personal behavior
_____ Not socially accepted by peers
_____ Poor self-esteem or self-image

Classroom illustrations of behaviors circled:

Conceptual-cognitive Behavior Difficulties

Ratings

_____ Poor logical reasoning and thinking
_____ Does not recognize class identities
_____ Not aware of current events
_____ Inadequate arithmetic reasoning
_____ Lacks basic arithmetic processes
_____ Poor number concepts
_____ Easily confused

Classroom illustrations of behaviors circled:

Language Behavior Difficulties

Ratings

_____ Poor spelling
_____ Problems in writing
_____ Limited reading comprehension
_____ Inadequate word attack skills
_____ Faulty articulation
_____ Limited verbal fluency—poor grammar
_____ Poor vocabulary

Classroom illustrations of behaviors circled:

Perceptual-motor Behavior Difficulties—Visual-motor

Ratings

_____ Poor coordination of eyes, hands, and large muscles
_____ Slow in completing tasks
_____ Clumsy in moving about room
_____ Tracing and drawing difficulties
_____ Trouble in drawing designs and symbols from memory

Classroom illustrations of behaviors circled:

Perceptual-motor Behavior Difficulties—Visual

Ratings

_____ Cannot verbally recall objects or materials removed from the environment
_____ Has trouble finding "hidden pictures" or little words in larger words
_____ Cannot match pictures or symbols
_____ Difficulty in coordinating and focusing eyes
_____ Problems in visual awareness and acuity

Classroom illustrations of behaviors circled:

Perceptual-motor Behavior Difficulties—Auditory

Ratings

_____ Cannot imitate specific sound patterns or noises
_____ Trouble in recalling what has been said to him
_____ Cannot associate to simple verbal opposites (up-down)
_____ Difficulty in following verbal instructions and directions
_____ Problems in hearing acuity

Classroom illustrations of behaviors circled:

Sensory-motor Behavior Difficulties

Ratings

_____ Problems in judging time and punctuality

_____ Not consistently right- or left-handed

_____ Confused in directions moving about school; disorganized

_____ Difficulty in identifying objects by touch and feel

_____ Poor attention or concentration span, distractible, hyperactive

_____ Trouble in imitating body movements or positions

_____ Poor balance, rhythm, agility

_____ Lethargy, nonresponsiveness

Classroom illustrations of behaviors circled:

Gross-motor Behavior Difficulties

Ratings

_____ Obviously poor physical health

_____ Lacks muscular strength and endurance

_____ Difficulty in locating and naming body parts

_____ Poor walking coordination

_____ Cannot crawl smoothly

_____ Poor sitting posture

_____ Cannot roll body in controlled manner

_____ Awkward in dancing

_____ Trouble in skipping

_____ Poor jumping

_____ Inadequate throwing and catching

_____ Problems in running and jogging

Classroom illustrations of behaviors circled:

Pupil Work Sample

This section is to be given individually to the pupil by the referring teacher, who should introduce it by saying: "We are going to play some easy games together to see how well you can follow directions and solve problems. Let's see how many of these you can do."

1. Touch your nose._____ 2. ears._____ 3. knees._____
4. ankles. _____
5. Throw this paper ball in the wastebasket. _____
6. Stand on one foot and jump over this book without falling. _____
7. Show me how you do a push-up. _____
8. Place your right hand on your left ear. _____
9. Place your left foot on your right foot. _____
10. Place your left hand on your right shoulder and your right hand on your left knee. _____
11. Stand like this:

    teacher _☘_ pupil _____ 12. teacher _☘_ pupil _____
13. Draw the letter T on the top of this page. _____
14. Draw the letter B on the bottom of this page. _____
15. Draw the letter R on the right side of this page. _____
16. What sound does a cat make? _____ 17. a dog make? _____
18. Does a bird sing? _____ 19. Does a car fly? _____
20. Repeat: A-5-T._____ 21. X-7-M-4. _____ 22. 3-C-O-6-Z. _____

Make an X on the one that looks like the first one.

23.	~	~	~~	~	~	~
24.	8 b	8 d	8 b	B d	8 d	B b
25.	☺	☺	☺	☺	☺	☺
26.	mdusp	mdsup	mbsup	mduzp	mdusp	mdnsp

A BASIC SCREENING AND REFERRAL FORM 27

Copy each design.

27. 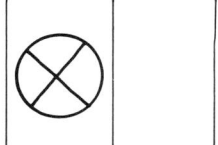 28.  29.

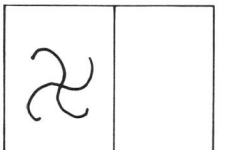

30. 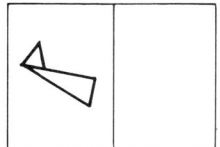 31. 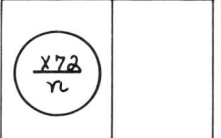 32.

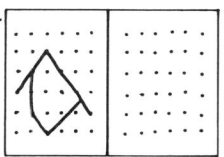

Tell me what letter, number, or word this is.

33. A   39. 9   45. CAT
34. P   40. 21   46. SCHOOL
35. Q   41. 300   47. FARM
36. J   42. 793   48. LETTER
37. R   43. BOY   49. APPLE
38. 5   44. AND   50 FATHER

51. Read this and then do what it says.

Draw ears, arms, a body, legs, and feet on the face. Then draw a box around your finished picture.

52. Print your A, B, C's. _____
   _____

53. Write your name and address. _____
   _____

54. When is your birthday? _____

55. When is Christmas? _____

Find the answers to these arithmetic exercises.

56.	57.	58.	59.	60.
4 +1	12 +9	5 +3	16 −8	3 ×2

61.	62.	63.	64.	65.
9 ×7	18 ×6	3)9	4)84	7)217

66. How many ounces in one pound of candy? _____

67. How many pints in a quart? _____

Complete these sentences as I read them to you.

68. What I like to do is _____
   _____

69. The thing that bothers me is _____
   _____

70. My friends are _____
   _____

71. I would like to learn _____
   _____

> If relevant, enclose a sample of this pupil's questionable classroom work with this referral.

Teacher Impressions and Suggestions

A. What do you feel this pupil needs to learn most at this time (priority objectives, etc.)?

B. How do you suggest this pupil might best be helped at this time?

C. Comments:

CHAPTER 5

Developmental task analysis

Child's name_____

Birth date_____

Date of this evaluation_____

Evaluated by_____

Relationship to child_____

The *Developmental Task Analysis* consists of 100 behavioral tasks that are basic to success in learning; most children accomplish practically all of these tasks by the middle elementary grades. Parents and others concerned can rate the child's accomplishment at a given time by marking an X in the appropriate column according to the following scale:

3 = Well learned with no difficulties.
2 = Partially learned with some difficulties.
1 = Beginning to be learned with many difficulties and little accomplishment.
0 = Has not begun to learn and rejects task.

Following completion of the Task Analysis, the evaluator should go back and underline those tasks presenting the most problems at this time. Comments and illustrations of special problems and concerns should then be written in the space provided.

Copyright, ©1969, by *Lear Siegler, Inc., Education Division / Fearon Publishers, 6 Davis Drive, Belmont, California 94002.* All rights reserved. No part of this form may be reproduced by any means, nor transmitted, nor translated into a machine language, without the written permission of the publisher.

LEARNING TASKS	0	1	2	3
SOCIAL AND PERSONAL SKILLS (relating to others)				
1. Is aware of self and of effect on others.				
2. Is aware of and responds to parents when present.				
3. Acknowledges friends and siblings.				
4. Does not demand unusual care and attention.				
5. Plays constructively by self with toys.				
6. Smiles and laughs when stimulated by others.				
7. Plays with other children and adults.				
8. Shares and cooperates in play.				
9. Plays simple competitive games with others.				
10. Cares for animals or other favorite objects.				
11. Helps with simple family chores and tasks.				
12. Attends to and completes various tasks.				
13. Demonstrates self-control (no temper tantrums).				
14. Has some special interests or hobbies.				
15. Has several friends and is popular with others.				
16. Is generally honest and straightforward.				
17. Has a sense of right and wrong that guides his behavior.				
18. Helps other people and shows empathy.				
19. Attends school full time.				
20. Participates in clubs, teams, or social groups.				
21. Is courteous and pleasant toward others.				
22. Assumes personal and social responsibility in family, school, and neighborhood.				
23. Accepts constructive criticism.				

Comments and Illustrations:

DEVELOPMENTAL TASK ANALYSIS

LEARNING TASKS	0	1	2	3
MOTOR SKILLS (body movement and control)				
24. Crawls across the floor without difficulty.				
25. Walks without aid or support.				
26. Walks up and down stairs.				
27. Can jump over small obstacles.				
28. Runs around the yard.				
29. Throws and catches rubber ball.				
30. Skips back and forth.				
31. Cares for self at toilet.				
32. Washes and bathes self.				
33. Dresses self.				
34. Ties shoes.				
35. Completes coloring book pictures with crayons.				
36. Cuts paper with blunt scissors.				
37. Jumps rope.				
38. Uses wagon and scooter.				
39. Rides bicycle.				
40. Uses skates.				
41. Participates in informal neighborhood or school sports.				
42. Moves about neighborhood or community without supervision.				
43. Participates in formal competitive athletics.				
Comments and Illustrations:				
PERCEPTUAL SKILLS (listening-seeing-doing)				
44. Plays with and responds to sound and musical toys.				
45. Replies appropriately to simple directions.				
46. Can repeat simple words, numbers, sentences.				
47. Can repeat a poem or simple song.				
48. Focuses eyes on picture or storybook (without notable difficulty).				

LEARNING TASKS	0	1	2	3
PERCEPTUAL SKILLS—Continued				
49. Can match duplicate pictures or playing cards.				
50. Has no knowledgeable visual disability or handicap.				
51. Uses knife, fork, and spoon at the table.				
52. Can match letters, numbers, and simple words.				
53. Knows ABC's by name when presented out of order.				
54. Draws recognizable figures and pictures with pencil.				
55. Prints name.				
56. Builds block houses.				
57. Assembles simple jigsaw puzzles.				
58. Writes ABC's.				
59. Writes numbers 1 to 30.				
60. Does *not* make reversals or write backward.				
61. Can quickly sort out different buttons.				
62. Ties knots in rope.				
63. Threads needle through buttonholes.				
64. *Writes* name with good handwriting.				
65. Uses hammer and nails and other tools.				
Comments and Illustrations:				
LANGUAGE SKILLS (vocabulary understanding and speech)				
66. Points to simple objects in pictures as requested.				
67. Imitates sounds and words.				
68. Has limited vocabulary.				
69. Talks in sentences.				
70. Describes events or objects with fluency.				
71. Can define simple words such as "hat," "apple," "letter."				
72. Explains simple arithmetic problems.				

DEVELOPMENTAL TASK ANALYSIS

LEARNING TASKS	0	1	2	3
LANGUAGE SKILLS—Continued				
73. Does *not* have articulation or other speech difficulties.				
74. Reads simple words.				
75. Spells simple words.				
76. Writes address and city.				
77. Reads appropriate school books.				
78. Writes simple letters and sentences.				
79. Uses telephone books and makes calls.				
80. Completes business applications.				
Comments and Illustrations:				
THINKING SKILLS (reasoning, judging, problem-solving) 81. Knows all human body parts.				
82. Knows basic colors.				
83. Remembers what happened yesterday.				
84. Can count pennies to 20.				
85. Knows nickel, dime, quarter.				
86. Can sort *big* and *little* sticks.				
87. Knows *top* and *bottom* of a box.				
88. Understands *in* and *out* of a bag.				
89. Knows *left* from *right*.				
90. Understands *loud* and *soft*.				
91. Knows months of the year.				
92. Knows the four seasons.				
93. Does simple addition.				
94. Does simple subtraction.				
95. Tells time to quarter hour.				
96. Does multiplication.				

LEARNING TASKS	0	1	2	3
THINKING SKILLS—Continued				
97. Understands jokes and/or riddles.				
98. Understands "city," "state," "nation."				
99. Purchases things at the store.				
100. Explains the rules of baseball or football.				

Comments and Illustrations:

For Professional Use and Recommendations:

Signed_____

CHAPTER 6

An inventory of primary skills

An Inventory of Primary Skills consists of 300 developmental learning tasks categorized into 19 areas. It was developed for parents to use in making a systematic observation of those tasks felt to be important in their child's learning. Teachers and other child specialists find it useful as part of a remedial training plan. The *Inventory* can be administered in whole or in part. The evaluator should tell the child that they are going to play some games and then proceed in a relaxed way. Although the child should be encouraged to respond to as many tasks as he can, the evaluator should not force him when he experiences difficulty. When presenting the alphabet and numbers, it is best to take them out of order. The evaluator should also make notes of pupil responses or comments that would be important to consider at a later time.

Child's name _____

Inventory date ___ ___ ___ (year month day)
Birthdate ___ ___ ___
Age ___ ___ ___

PAGE	TASK DESCRIPTION	TOTAL NUMBER OF TASKS	NUMBER COMPLETED	PAGE	TASK DESCRIPTION	TOTAL NUMBER OF TASKS	NUMBER COMPLETED
2	Self information	11		5	Copying house	1	
	Body identification	15			Draw-a-man	1	
	Body spatial relations	4			Sight vocabulary	40	
3	Copying designs	14			Paragraph reading	2	
	Alphabet printing	26		6–8	Alphabet knowledge	26	
	Writing numbers	31		9	Number knowledge	10	
4	Symbol matching	5		10–11	Class concepts	14	
	Sentence copying	6		12–13	Position in space concepts	42	
	Counting	3		14–15	Descriptive concepts	36	
	Basic arithmetic	12			TOTAL	299	

Attention and motivation:

Physical limitations:

Apparent strengths:

Apparent weaknesses:

Comments and recommendations:

Signature _____ Date _____

Copyright, © 1970, by Fearon Publishers/Lear Siegler, Inc., Education Division.

Write your name.	
Write *(or tell me)* your birth date.	
Write *(or tell me)* your address.	
Write *(or tell me)* what city and state you live in.	
Write *(or tell me)* your telephone number.	
Write *(or tell me)* the name of your school.	
Write *(or tell me)* the name of your teacher and your class.	
Write *(or tell me)* what date this is.	
Write *(or tell me)* mother's first name and father's first name.	

Follow my directions. (Score + or −) Touch your: head_____ ears_____ eyes_____ nose_____ mouth_____ feet_____ hips_____ elbows_____ ankles_____ shoulders_____

Show me your: left foot_____ right hand_____ right ear_____ left eye_____ right foot_____

Watch me and stand exactly the way I am:

Parent Child	Parent Child	Parent Child	Parent Child

AN INVENTORY OF PRIMARY SKILLS

Copy each design in the space provided.

Print the alphabet.

Write numbers through 31.

On pages 6–9 are some large shaded alphabet letters and numbers. First present the alphabet letters by pointing to one at a time and saying, "What is this?" For each correct response place a + mark below the letter. Repeat the same procedure for the numbers. Indicate results below. *(Note: Do this task first, before continuing with the tasks below.)*

No. of letters correct. _____ No. of numbers correct. _____

Put an × by the one that looks like the first one. (Give example if necessary.)

Mm	Mw	Mm	Wm	Ww	mM
was	saw	was	sam	mas	wsa

Copy this sentence. *The big dog chased the boy.*

How many apples? _____	How many cats? _____	How many boys? _____

$$3 \quad 11 \quad 9 \quad 26 \quad 5 \quad 9 \quad 16 \quad 213$$
$$\underline{+2} \quad \underline{+4} \quad \underline{-3} \quad \underline{-17} \quad \underline{\times 3} \quad \underline{\times 7} \quad \underline{\times 4} \quad \underline{\times 4}$$

$$4\overline{)8} \qquad 3\overline{)12} \qquad 7\overline{)231} \qquad 4\overline{)\$2.04}$$

AN INVENTORY OF PRIMARY SKILLS 41

Copy the house.

Draw a man.

Sight vocabulary: "Tell me each word as I point to it." (Underline if correct and write in other responses.)

boy	in	big	and	to
we	ball	go	cat	him
is	good	two	yes	ran
under	over	soon	after	where
school	horse	pull	farm	read
bird	was	house	you	apple
they	coat	cut	father	please
window	open	letter	always	picture

Read me these stories. (Underline if read correctly, and write in other responses.)

The Ball

The boy had a big red ball. He would throw it to his dog. His dog was named King. King would catch the ball.

Cats

Many people love cats and keep them as pets. Most cats like to catch mice.

When cats are very small, they are called kittens. Little kittens are soft and cute.

LEARNING DISABILITIES

a b c
d e f
g h i

j k l
m n o
p q r

stu
vwx
yz

AN INVENTORY OF PRIMARY SKILLS

1234
567
890

Class concepts: "Place your finger on the _____." (Mark + for each correct response and – for each incorrect response. Record if child refused to attempt task.)

1. _____ Boys
2. _____ Girls
3. _____ Animals
   (bird, cat, snake)
4. _____ People
   (boys, girls)
5. _____ Food
   (apple, bread, ice cream)
6. _____ Clothes
   (shirt, shoes, pants)
7. _____ Furniture
   (chair, table, bed)
8. _____ Tools
   (hammer, saw, screwdriver)

AN INVENTORY OF PRIMARY SKILLS 47

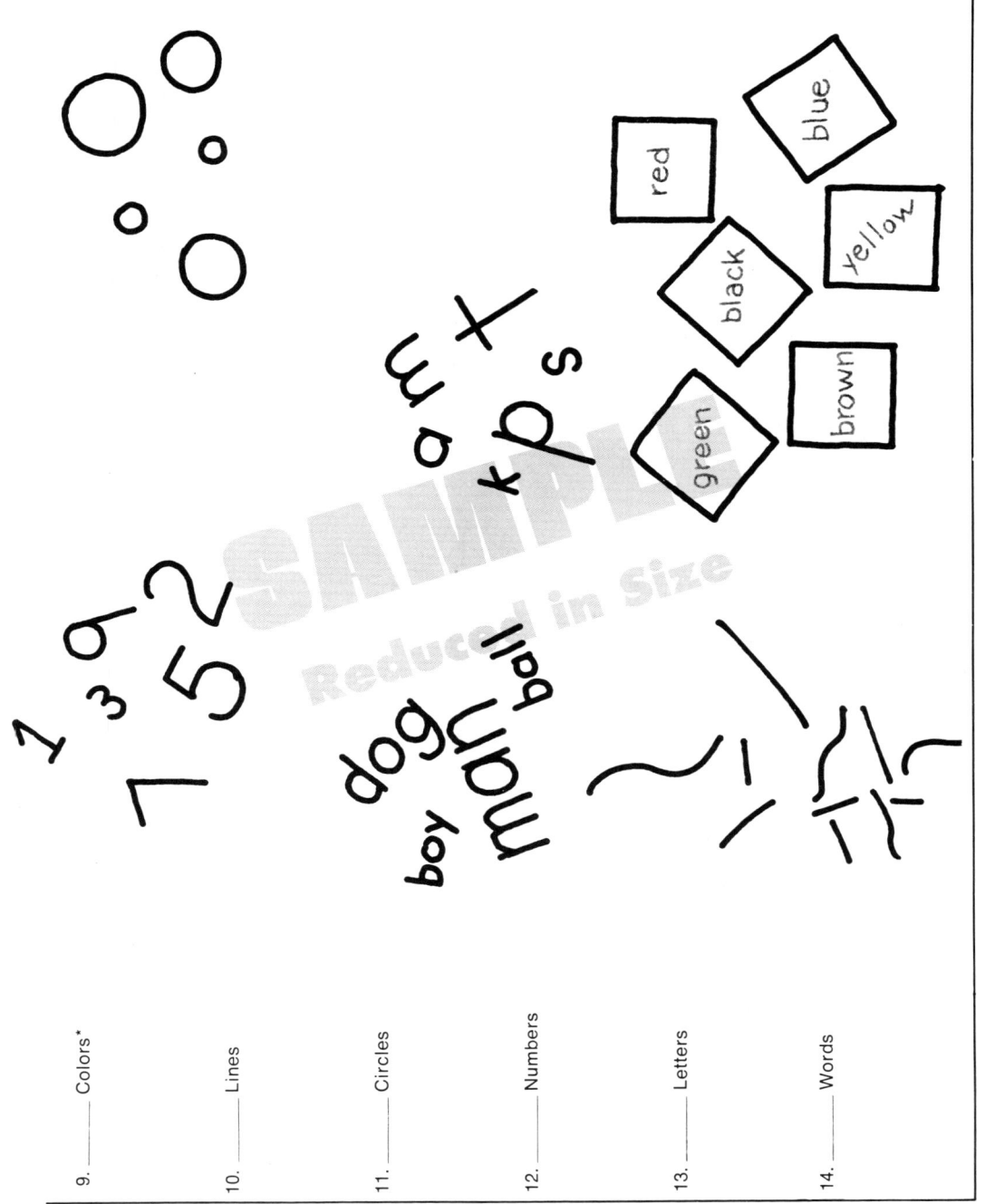

9. _____ Colors*

10. _____ Lines

11. _____ Circles

12. _____ Numbers

13. _____ Letters

14. _____ Words

* Color in the shapes before evaluating child.

Position in space concepts: "Point to the (first) (boy)." (Mark + for each correct response and − for each incorrect response. Record if child refused to attempt task.)	
boys—cats 1. _____ First 2. _____ Last 3. _____ Middle	
bird—balloon 4. _____ On 5. _____ Over 6. _____ Under	
cat—girl 7. _____ In 8. _____ Out	
plane—kite 9. _____ Up 10. _____ Down	

AN INVENTORY OF PRIMARY SKILLS   49

boy—girl 11. _____ Front 12. _____ Back	
boys—girls 13. _____ In front 14. _____ Behind		
cats 15. _____ Above 16. _____ Below		
box—flagpole—dresser 17. _____ Top 18. _____ Bottom	
hands—feet 19. _____ Left 20. _____ Right	

50   LEARNING DISABILITIES

Descriptive concepts: "Place your finger on the (big) things." (Mark + for each correct response and − for each incorrect response. Record if child refuses to attempt task.)

1. _____ Big
2. _____ Little

3. _____ Hot
4. _____ Cold

5. _____ Fast
6. _____ Slow

7. _____ Light
8. _____ Dark

AN INVENTORY OF PRIMARY SKILLS   51

9. ____ Loud
10. ____ Soft

11. ____ Long
12. ____ Short

13. ____ Few
14. ____ Many

15. ____ Alike
16. ____ Different

CHAPTER 7
The psychoeducational inventory of basic learning abilities

A Psychoeducational Inventory of Basic Learning Abilities has been developed as an aid in the initial evaluation of elementary and junior high pupils with suspected learning disabilities. The *Inventory* has been designed for special education teachers, remedial specialists, educational therapists and consultants, psychologists, and others concerned with the learning problems of children. Its major use is with exceptional children for whom highly specific instruction must be devised.

The *Inventory* samples educational tasks from fifty-three basic learning abilities that have been grouped into six major areas of learning: gross motor development, sensory-motor integration, perceptual-motor skills, language development, conceptual skills, and social skills. It is anticipated that the *Inventory* will be used for pupil placement in, or recommendation for, some type of special education class or educational therapy. The basic assumption is that the teacher of children with learning disabilities must begin with an evaluation of major educational tasks as a prerequisite to any meaningful curriculum development or remedial plan. The tasks should always be administered in an individual situation. The *Inventory* is not a standardized instrument; it relies entirely on the examiner's subjective judgment and experience regarding the rating to be employed and the nature of the remedial program required. It will be most helpful when used by the teacher in conjunction with a psychoeducational consultant, such as a school psychologist, who can follow up on the *Inventory* with more specialized examinations if needed. For purposes of educational planning, the author's handbook, *The Remediation of Learning Disabilities* (Fearon Publishers), is recommended for specific programming of the basic learning abilities.

MATERIALS REQUIRED

Specific instructions for the evaluation of each educational task are contained in the *Inventory*. The accompanying *Workbook* provides space for all pencil and paper responses. The following materials should be obtained to complete the examiner's kit: teaspoon; bead; texture ball; old newspapers for paper balls; softball; jump rope; contemporary records and record player; hand mirror; brick; playing cards; books; paper bag; nail, stick, and pencil; two-inch-long stick, four-inch-long stick, and six-inch-long stick; wood, plastic, or cardboard letters (A-B-N-M-Y-X-T); square wood building block; scissors; cardboard paper towel roll from which to make a telescope; card (big enough to cover eye) with hole in it; yardstick; wristwatch; thumbtack; picture; six coins; half-inch bolts, washers, and nuts (three of each).

RATINGS

The pupil's response to each educational task should be noted under the column headed "Notes," and a check mark or X should be placed immediately in the appropriate rating column. Tasks are listed by level of difficulty: B—beginning tasks that are generally accomplished by children in primary grades, ages five to eight; M—middle-level tasks that are successfully performed by middle elementary pupils, ages eight to ten; and A—advanced tasks that are generally accomplished by upper elementary pupils, ages ten to twelve. Actual ratings should be checked in one of the five columns according to the following scale:

1. VW—*very weak performance.* Very little, if any, actual task achievement. Poor attention and concentration, very little effort demonstrated, little or no response or skill evident.
2. W—*weak performance.* Limited skill or response, obvious difficulty in attending to task, cautious, unsure, lacking confidence.
3. A—*average performance.* Partial accomplishment judged appropriate for mental and physiological development.
4. S—*strong performance.* Fairly good task achievement, quite responsive, confident, no lack of attention.
5. VS—*very strong performance.* High achievement and response, excellent motivation, effortless performance.

ADMINISTRATION

Since the basic learning abilities in the *Psychoeducational Inventory* are presented in approximate developmental order, it is usually not necessary to administer all of the tasks to all children. Young children are expected to be more successful on the beginning tasks and to experience increasing difficulty on the middle and advanced tasks. Therefore, parts of the *Inventory* should be selected as beginning points for evaluation according to the age of the child. The following "starting points" are recommended for examiner consideration:

Grade	Pupil's Age	Task Number	Starting Level
Preschool	3–5	Gross Motor 1	B
K	5–6	Gross Motor 1	M
1	6–7	Gross Motor 4	M
2	7–8	Gross Motor 6	M
3	8–9	Sensory Motor 15	M
4	9–10	Sensory Motor 19	B
5	10–11	Perceptual Motor 22	M
6	11–12	Perceptual Motor 26	M
7	13 and older	Perceptual Motor 30	A

If the pupil successfully completes the starting task indicated above, move on to the next more advanced task and then go to the next learning ability. For example, if an 8½-year-old child starts with task 6M and successfully passes it, give task 6A next; if 6A is failed, go back and give 6B. Then proceed to task 7M and continue accordingly.

Children with obvious learning disabilities should be started on Gross Motor Development 1 at the beginning task level so that they have every opportunity to succeed wherever possible. The Inventory should be given in sections or parts as judged necessary. Each of the six levels (Gross Motor Development, Sensory-Motor Integration, Perceptual Motor Skills, Language Development, Conceptual Skills, and Social Skills) should be given separately if feasible. At no time should more than fifty or sixty minutes be spent in continual evaluation. It must be remembered that this is a teacher-diagnostician criterion instrument and not a standardized test; therefore, the examiner should feel free to modify or supplement any of the tasks presented but should carefully note these together with any unique comments or responses from the pupil.

INDIVIDUAL PROFILES

Following use of the *Inventory,* it is essential that the results be profiled and summarized for educational planning. This can be done in a number of different ways. A common approach is to begin with a review of the evaluator's rating for each learning ability and to judge the pupil's total performance on the tasks administered. For example, Alex, an eleven-year-old boy with many learning problems, was administered most tasks from the *Inventory;* on Visual Form Discrimination No. 29, he was given the middle and advanced tasks and responded quickly and accurately and was therefore checked in the "very strong" column on the profile sheet (Figure 4). However, he experienced increasing difficulty with Language Development and Conceptual Skills; on Classification

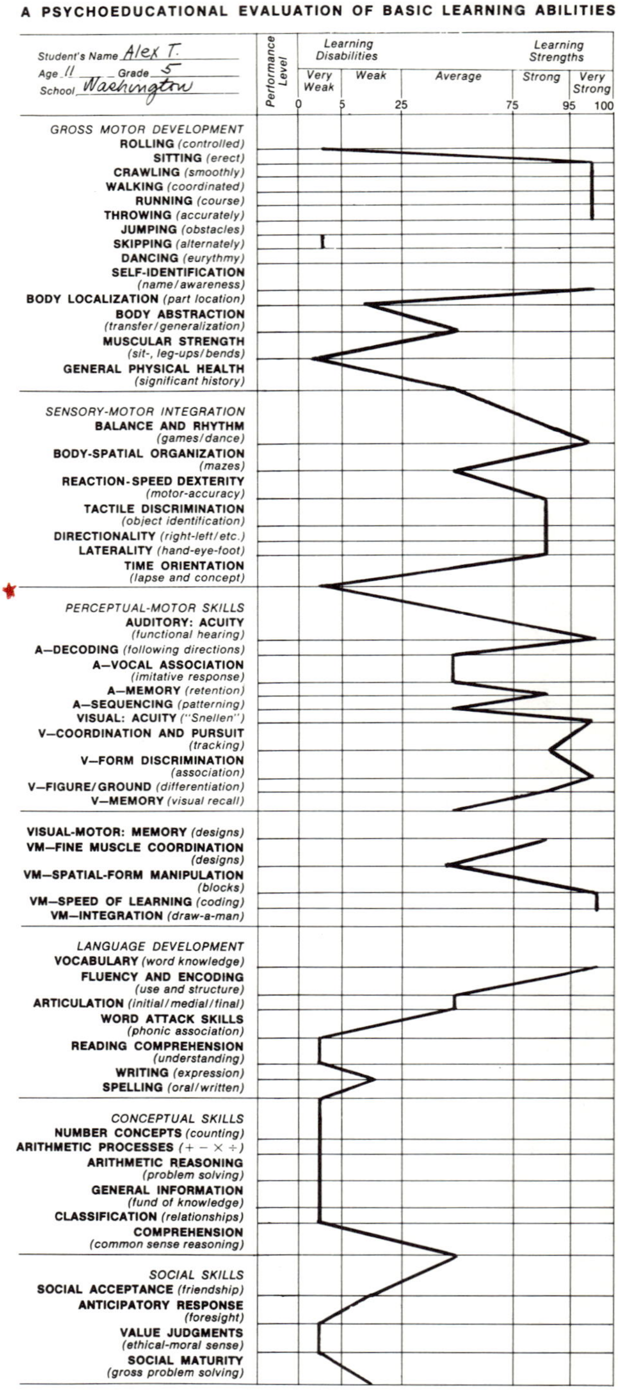

Figure 4.
A performance profile

| BASIC LEARNING ABILITIES INVENTORY SUMMARY |
| AND PRESCRIPTIVE IMPLICATIONS |

Pupil's Name_____ Birthdate_____

School_____ Age_____

Diagnostic Evaluator_____ Dates Evaluated_____

Basic Learning Abilities	Learning Strengths	Learning Disabilities
SOCIAL SKILLS		
CONCEPTUAL SKILLS		
LANGUAGE SKILLS		
PERCEPTUAL-MOTOR SKILLS		
SENSORY-MOTOR SKILLS		
GROSS MOTOR SKILLS		

Recommended Priority Teaching Objective:

Recommended Prescriptive Learning
Tasks & Strategies:

Comments:

Figure 5.

No. 48, he was presented all beginning, middle, and advanced tasks and reacted with confusion, failure, and frustration on all levels. Therefore, his overall performance on this ability was judged to be "very weak" and this was marked on his profile.

When the *Inventory* ratings have been moved to the pupil's profile form (Figure 4), their implications for prescriptive learning can then be considered and summarized. This is most simply done through use of the Basic Learning Abilities Inventory Summary and Prescriptive Implications form (Figure 5). The diagnostic teacher-evaluator writes in the specific learning strengths and the weaknesses judged to be disabilities. These are then considered in terms of teaching objectives and procedures, which are then indicated on the bottom of the form.

The form then becomes a guide for specification of learning objectives and teaching recommendations. Another type of summary which emphasizes specific

```
Mr. Bradford    of  Alex T.        at  Washington      on  11/14/72
  Teacher         Pupil's Name          School              Date
```

RECOMMENDED PSYCHOEDUCATIONAL PROGRAMS AND MATERIALS

GROSS MOTOR DEVELOPMENT

( ) 1. Rolling
( ) 2. Sitting
( ) 3. Crawling
( ) 4. Walking
( ) 5. Running
( ) 6. Throwing
( ) 7. Jumping
( ) 8. Skipping
( ) 9. Dancing
( ) 10. Self-Identification
( ) 11. Body Localization
( ) 12. Body Abstraction
√(2c) 13. Muscular Strength
( ) 14. General Physical Health

SENSORY-MOTOR INTEGRATION

( ) 15. Balance & Rhythm
( ) 16. Body-Spatial Organization
( ) 17. Reaction-Speed Dexterity
( ) 18. Tactile Discrimination
( ) 19. Directionality
( ) 20. Laterality
√(3d) 21. Time Orientation

PERCEPTUAL-MOTOR SKILLS

( ) 22. Auditory Acuity
( ) 23. Auditory Decoding
( ) 24. Auditory-vocal Association
( ) 25. Auditory Memory
( ) 26. Auditory Sequencing
( ) 27. Visual Acuity
( ) 28. Visual Coordination & Pursuit
( ) 29. Visual-Form Discrimination
( ) 30. Visual Figure-Ground Differentiation
( ) 31. Visual Memory
( ) 32. Visual-Motor Memory
√(3b) 33. Visual-Motor Fine Muscle Coordination
( ) 34. Visual-Motor Spatial-Form Manipulation
( ) 35. Visual-Motor Speed of Learning
( ) 36. Visual-Motor Integration

LANGUAGE DEVELOPMENT

( ) 37. Vocabulary
( ) 38. Fluency and Encoding
( ) 39. Articulation
√(2c) 40. Word Attack Skills
( ) 41. Reading Comprehension
( ) 42. Writing
( ) 43. Spelling

CONCEPTUAL SKILLS

( ) 44. Number Concepts
( ) 45. Arithmetic Processes
( ) 46. Arithmetic Reasoning
( ) 47. General Information
√(3a)b 48. Classification
( ) 49. Comprehension

SOCIAL SKILLS

( ) 50. Social Acceptance
( ) 51. Anticipatory Response
√(1b) (52). Value Judgment
( ) 53. Social Maturity

OTHER PRESCRIPTIVE RECOMMENDATIONS:

Provide Alex with more opportunities to discuss his social-personal problems with classmates as part of the daily class meeting session.

Figure 6. Should you have access to Valett's *Remediation of Learning Disabilities** handbook for teachers, the above check-marked items purport to, if diligently applied, strengthen this pupil in those areas of his growth and development that have been indicated by this evaluation as being less than is expected for his age attainment. Priority consideration should be given to encircled numbers.

learning tasks for prescriptive teaching is the Recommended Psychoeducational Programs and Materials form (Figure 6). In the illustration given, a number of specific learning tasks from *The Remediation of Learning Disabilities* have been listed for immediate teacher consideration.

Individual performance profiles can be used to show progress toward selected learning task objectives also. For greater accuracy, the diagnostic teacher first

---

*Valett, Robert, *The Remediation of Learning Disabilities, A Handbook of Psychoeducational Resource Programs,* Fearon Publishers/Lear Siegler, Inc., Education Division, 6 Davis Drive, Belmont, California 94002.

marks the rating scale columns of the *Psychoeducational Inventory of Basic Learning Abilities* in black, then adds the midyear or final *Inventory* ratings in red. This clearly indicates what progress has been made on any beginning, middle, or advanced learning tasks selected. If desired, ratings can be quantified for scoring or research purposes by using a one-to-five scale; a "very weak" rating receives one point, and a "very strong" rating receives five points. Although reevaluation summary ratings might also be marked in different colors on a performance profile, it is more meaningful to use the actual *Inventory* booklet itself for this purpose when changes in specific learning tasks are clearly evident.

GROUP PROFILING

The *Psychoeducational Inventory* can also be summarized and profiled on a small-group or class basis. This may be helpful in planning instructional activities for small groups of children with similar kinds of learning disorders. For example, the *Inventory* can be divided into several parts or sections. Perceptual-Motor Skills, Part I (Figure 7) illustrates the format recommended for profiling a group of pupils. This then allows comparison of learning strengths and disabilities as judged by the diagnostic teacher for scheduling and programming purposes.

Classes may also be profiled on the *Psychoeducational Inventory of Basic Learning Abilities*. A school profile for twenty fourth-grade pupils is presented

PERCEPTUAL MOTOR SKILLS (PART I)																																			
PUPILS' NAMES	AUDITORY ACUITY					AUDITORY DECODING					A - VOCAL ASSOCIATION					AUDITORY MEMORY					AUDITORY SEQUENCING					VISUAL ACUITY					VISUAL COORDINATION AND PURSUIT				
RATINGS	VW	W	A	S	VS	VW	W	A	S	VS	VW	W	A	S	VS	VW	W	A	S	VS	VW	W	A	S	VS	VW	W	A	S	VS	VW	W	A	S	VS

Figure 7.

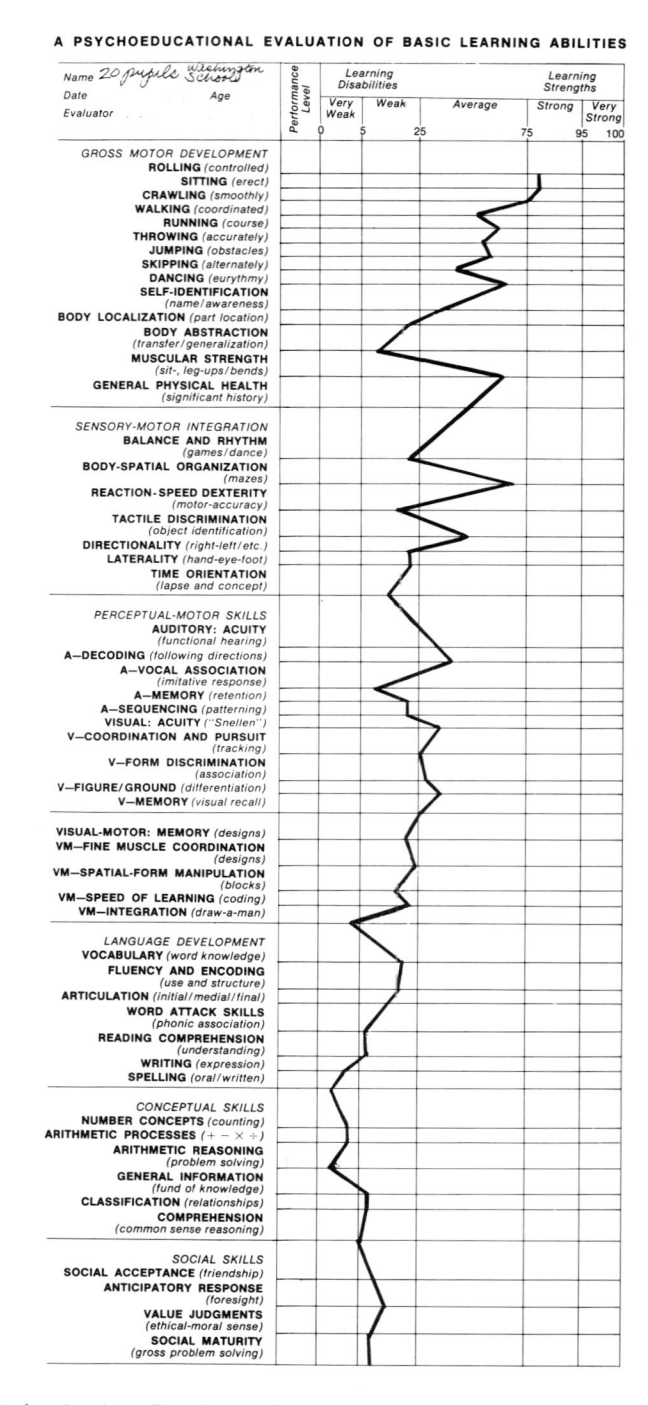

Figure 8. A school profile of basic learning abilities for twenty pupils.

in Figure 8. The average chronological age for this group was ten years, but the average grade placement in reading was low second grade. The profile reflects relatively good performance in the gross motor and sensory-motor skills and shows increasing difficulty with perceptual, conceptual, and social skills and abilities. This is a typical profile showing developmental difficulties for children with learning disorders. In this particular school, careful attention might be given to the organization of priority small group prescriptive programs in such learning skills as time orientation, auditory vocal association, visual-motor integration, reading comprehension, spelling, and arithmetic reasoning. Of course individual prescriptive programs are an essential part of any supplemental group instruction and should always be given first consideration by the teacher.

THE INVENTORY AND WORKBOOK

The actual *Inventory* follows below. A *Workbook* to accompany the *Inventory* is also included. These materials are best used as part of a broader evaluation using other instruments presented in this book.

```
Pupil's name_____

Address_____

School_____

Class or program_____

Age_____

Birth date_____
                mo.          day          yr.
Date beginning
Inventory_____
                mo.          day          yr.


Examiner_____
```

Copyright, ©1968, by **Lear Siegler, Inc., Education Division / Fearon Publishers, 6 Davis Drive, Belmont, California 94002.** All rights reserved. No part of this book may be reproduced in any form without permission in writing from the publishers.

A Psychoeducational Inventory of Basic Learning Abilities

Robert E. Valett, Ed.D.
Professor of Education, California State University, Fresno, and Consulting Psychologist.

Age _____
Birth date _____ mo. _____ day _____ yr.
Date beginning Inventory _____ mo. _____ day _____ yr.
Examiner _____

Pupil's name _____
Address _____
School _____
Class or program _____

Copyright ©1968 by Lear Siegler, Inc. / Fearon Publishers, 6 Davis Drive, Belmont, California 94002.

ISBN-0-8224-5640-0

Lear Siegler, Inc./Fearon Publishers
Belmont, California

SAMPLE
Reduced in Size

THE PSYCHOEDUCATIONAL INVENTORY OF BASIC LEARNING ABILITIES

GROSS MOTOR DEVELOPMENT: The development and awareness of large muscle activity. (Basic learning abilities 1-14)

Learning Ability	Illustration	Task Level	Specific Learning Task (The examiner should give the following directions to the pupil.)	Notes	Rating Scale VW W A S VS
1. **Rolling:** The ability to roll one's body in a controlled manner.	From a supine position, with arms over head, pupil can roll from back to stomach. Pupil can do sequential rolling to right and left, can roll down hill or incline.	B	Lie on your back with your arms over your head and your feet together. Roll over slowly to the right. Now roll over slowly to the left.		
		M	Put one arm straight over your head and the other arm down by your side. Roll to the right three times. Now roll to the left two times.		
		A	Do a forward somersault.		
2. **Sitting:** The ability to sit erect in a normal position without support or constant reminding.	Pupil can demonstrate proper poise in sitting at desk with feet on floor, back straight, and head and arms in proper position for work at hand.	B	Sit up straight with your feet flat on the floor and your hands folded while you count to ten.		
		M	Sit on the floor Indian-style, with your legs crossed and your arms folded, while you count to ten.		
		A	Sit up straight in your chair and let me see how long you can balance a book on your head.	Time:	
3. **Crawling:** The ability to crawl on hands and knees in a smooth and coordinated way.	With eyes fixated on target, pupil first crawls in a homolateral fashion. Pupil progresses to cross-lateral crawling program.	B	Crawl on the floor moving your arm and leg on the same side together (homolateral).		
		M	Crawl on the floor fast like a dog, moving your opposite arm and leg together (cross-lateral).		
		A	Crawl over to the wall while carrying this spoon with the bead on it between your teeth without dropping the bead.		
4. **Walking:** The ability to walk erect in a coordinated fashion without support.	With head up and shoulders back, pupil walks a specified path and walking line. Pupil can walk backward and sideways without difficulty.	B	Walk forward in a straight line putting one foot directly in front of the other. Touch the heel of one foot to the toes of the other.		
		M	Now walk backward in the same way, holding your arms out. Be sure your heels and toes are touching.		
		A	Now close your eyes, put your arms out in front of you, and walk straight to me. Remember to keep your eyes closed. (Pupil should not touch heel and toes as he walks.)		

Learning Ability	Illustration	Task Level	Specific Learning Task (The examiner should give the following directions to the pupil.)	Notes	Rating Scale VW W A S VS
5. **Running:** The ability to run a track or obstacle course without a change of pace.	Pupil runs a straight track of easy distance without difficulty, can change direction through a simple obstacle course without stopping or significantly changing pace.	B	Run in place while I count out loud to 50.		
		M	Run around the room (or obstacle course) without falling or bumping into anything.		
		A	Run from there to here (about 50 yards) as fast as you can.		
6. **Throwing:** The ability to throw a ball with a reasonable degree of accuracy.	Pupil throws a ball to another person so that it may be caught, can throw ball accurately into box or basket.	B	Throw this texture ball to me so that I can catch it.		
		M	Throw these three paper balls into the wastebasket from here. (Distance is approximately four feet.)		
		A	Let's play catch with this softball. (Pupil should catch and throw accurately three out of five times.)		
7. **Jumping:** The ability to jump simple obstacles without falling.	Pupil can jump from chair to floor without difficulty, can jump from jumping board without falling, can jump over knee-high obstacles.	B	Jump back and forth over this line three times.		
		M	Jump rope forward.		
		A	Jump rope backward.		
8. **Skipping:** The ability to skip in normal play.	Pupil can skip, alternating feet, around circle of players, can skip rope forward both by hopping and alternate-foot skipping.	B	Skip forward in a circle as I am doing.		
		M	Skip backward in a circle as I am doing.		
		A	Skip rope forward around in a circle.		
9. **Dancing:** The ability to move one's body in coordinated response to music.	In young children, abilities are shown by free movement and eurhythmic expression. There is a progression to more formal dance steps with older pupils.	B	March in a circle and slap your sides as I clap my hands.		
		M	Dance freely to the record I am going to play. (Play music such as The Nutcracker Suite.)		
		A	Do any modern dance for me when I play this record. (Play any contemporary record.)		
10. **Self-identification:** The ability to identify one's self.	Pupil can identify self by name, respond to name when called, and identify self in pictures and mirrors.	B	What is your name?		
		M	Point to yourself in this mirror. (Hand mirror should reflect part of the examiner and part of the pupil.)		
		A	I am printing three names on this paper. Point to your name. (Space provided in Workbook for response.)		

THE PSYCHOEDUCATIONAL INVENTORY OF BASIC LEARNING ABILITIES 65

Learning Ability	Illustration	Task Level	Specific Learning Task (The examiner should give the following directions to the pupil.)	Notes	Rating Scale VW W A S VS
11. **Body Localization:** The ability to locate parts of one's body.	Pupil can locate eyes, hands, mouth, hair, nose, feet, eyebrows, fingernails, shoulders, elbows, knees, back, neck, chin, forehead, wrists, arms, legs, toes.	B	Touch your eyes, nose, mouth, feet, and wrists.		
		M	Look in this mirror and point to your hair, teeth, eyebrows, and chin.		
		A	What are your eyes for? What are your hands for? What is your stomach for?		
12. **Body Abstraction:** The ability to transfer and generalize self-concepts and body localization.	Pupil can identify others by names and pictures, can locate body parts on others, generalize to pictures, complete body picture puzzles.	B	Point to the clown's nose, hands, feet, knees, hair, and elbows (see Workbook).		
		M	Draw a picture of yourself in this space (see Workbook). Draw your whole body. (Cover clown's picture in 12B.)		
		A	When you grow up, what do you think you will look like?		
13. **Muscular Strength:** The ability to use one's muscles to perform physical tasks.	Pupil can touch floor from standing position. From supine position he can sit up and touch toes, can raise legs off floor for few seconds. Pupil can do one push-up and chin self from bar.	B	Crouch down like this (demonstrate), and when I say "go," jump up and reach over your head.		
		M	Stand up with your feet together and raise your hands over your head. Now bend over and touch the floor.		
		A	Do one or two push-ups.		
14. **General Physical Health:** The ability to understand and apply principles of health and hygiene while demonstrating good general health.	Pupil has good personal health and hygiene habits—no chronic absences for health reasons, no unusual accidents or health history, and no significant physical disabilities interfering with learning.	B	What should you do if you cut your finger?		
		M	Tell me what foods should be in a balanced dinner.		
		A	Why is it important for boys and girls to get lots of exercise and sleep?		

SENSORY-MOTOR INTEGRATION: The psychophysical integration of fine and gross motor activities. (Basic learning abilities 15-21)

15. **Balance and Rhythm:** The ability to maintain gross and fine motor balance and to move rhythmically.	Pupil is able to balance on balance board or rail, can move rhythmically in playing jacks and in bouncing on trampoline or spring.	B	Stand on your tiptoes and run in a circle.		
		M	Walk forward and then backward along this line (or balance beam).		
		A	Balance yourself on one foot while standing on this brick.		

Learning Ability	Illustration	Task Level	Specific Learning Task (The examiner should give the following directions to the pupil.)	Notes	Rating Scale VW W A S VS
16. **Body-spatial Organization:** The ability to move one's body in an integrated way around and through objects in the spatial environment.	Pupil can run maze on playground or in classroom without bumping, can move easily through tunnels and use playground monkey bars, can imitate body positions in space.	B	Climb up on this chair and squat like the figure in this picture (see Workbook).		
		M	Crawl through my legs without touching me.		
		A	Stand up and move your arms and legs as I am doing.		
17. **Reaction-Speed Dexterity:** The ability to respond efficiently to general directions or assignments.	Pupil can attend to the teacher sufficiently to comprehend total directions. He can organize self and respond adequately to complete the given assignment within a normal time expectancy. Pupil has good attention and concentration span.	B	Make as many marks like this (/) in this box (see Workbook) as fast as you can until I tell you to stop. (Allow 60 seconds.)		
		M	Take this deck of cards. Turn all of the cards face up and group them together by aces, twos, threes, etc. Do this as fast as you can.	Time:	
		A	Go to that table and bring that book over here and open it to page 56 and point to the second paragraph on the page.	Time:	
18. **Tactile Discrimination:** The ability to identify and match objects by touching and feeling.	With hidden toys and materials, pupil can match objects with both left and right hands, name or classify materials or substances, differentiate weights, discriminate temperatures.	B	Put your hand in the bag and give me the nail. (Bag contains nail, stick, and pencil.)		
		M	Put your hand in the bag and give me the longest stick. (Bag contains 2"-long, 4"-long, and 6"-long sticks.)		
		A	Put your hand in the bag and give me the letter "A." Now give me the letter "X." (Bag contains A-B-N-M-Y-X-T.)		
19. **Directionality:** The ability to know right from left, up from down, forward from backward, and directional orientation.	Pupil can write and follow picture story or reading material from left to right, discriminate right and left body parts and those of other people, locate directions in room and school.	B	Touch the floor with your right hand. Now shake your left foot.		
		M	Put your finger on the bottom of this block. Now put your finger on the right side of the block. Now the top. Now the left side. (Use square wood building block.)		
		A	Point to the north, the south, the east, the west.		

THE PSYCHOEDUCATIONAL INVENTORY OF BASIC LEARNING ABILITIES

Learning Ability	Illustration	Task Level	Specific Learning Task (The examiner should give the following directions to the pupil.)	Notes	Rating Scale VW W A S VS
20. **Laterality:** The ability to integrate one's sensory-motor contact with the environment through establishment of homolateral hand, eye, and foot dominance.	Pupil has consistent right- or left-sided approach in use of eyes, hands, and feet in tasks such as kicking ball, cutting paper, sighting with telescope.	hand	Hand me that pencil. Cut this paper in two. Print your first name here (see Workbook).		
		foot	Kick this paper ball. Hop across the floor on one foot. Push this brick to the wall using one foot.		
		eye	Look out the window with this cardboard telescope. Look through the hole in this card and find the pencil in my hand. Pretend that this yardstick is a rifle and show me how you would hold it and sight it to shoot a lion.		
21. **Time Orientation:** The ability to judge lapses in time and to be aware of time concepts.	Pupil is prompt in attending class, completing timed assignments, and following directions. Child is aware of day, month, year, time of day, and seasons.	B	Jump up and down as I clap my hands.		
		M	What time of the year does Christmas come? _____ Easter? _____ Halloween? _____		
		A	What time is it by this watch?		
PERCEPTUAL-MOTOR SKILLS: The functional utilization of primary auditory, visual, and visual-motor skills. (Basic learning abilities 22-36)
22. **Auditory Acuity:** The ability to receive and differentiate auditory stumuli.	Pupil responds functionally to watch tick, hidden sound toys, and general normal conversational directions. Pupil has no significant decibel loss.	B	Listen to this watch tick when I place it by each of your ears. As I move it away, raise your hand when you no longer hear it.		
		M	Turn your back and listen. When I am through, turn around and repeat what I did. (Tap on desk three times; cough quietly twice.)		
		A	Turn your back, listen carefully, and then repeat what I whisper. ("I like chocolate ice cream." "What day is it today?")		
23. **Auditory Decoding:** The ability to understand sounds or spoken words.	Pupil can follow simple verbal instructions, can indicate by gesture or words the meaning or purpose of auditory stimuli such as animal sounds, nouns, or verbs.	B	Point to the appropriate picture (see Workbook) as I make the sound: "meow," "choo-choo," "moo."		
		M	Answer "Yes" or "No": Do cars move? _____ Is Billy a girl? _____ Can a tree grow? _____		
		A	Color the top part of the number 8, and then draw a line from 8 to 1 without touching the number 5 (see Workbook).		

	Learning Ability	Illustration	Task Level	Specific Learning Task (The examiner should give the following directions to the pupil.)	Notes	Rating Scale vW W A S vS
24.	**Auditory-vocal Association:** The ability to respond verbally in a meaningful way to auditory stimuli.	Pupil can associate with verbal opposites, sentence completions, or analogous verbal responses.	B	Tell me all the things you think of when you hear the word "vacation."		
			M	Which of the following does not belong: "John, Mary, Bill, George"?		
			A	Describe the clothes I have on.		
25.	**Auditory Memory:** The ability to retain and recall general auditory information.	Pupil can act out (charades) Santa Claus, simple plots of common nursery rhymes ("Jack and Jill"), can verbally relate yesterday's experiences, meals, television and story plots.	B	What is the title of your favorite song?		
			M	Tell me the sound a snake makes: _____; a train makes: _____; a sheep makes: _____.		
			A	Tell me your favorite story so that I can understand what it is about.		
26.	**Auditory Sequencing:** The ability to recall in correct sequence and detail prior auditory information.	Pupil can imitate specific sound patterns, follow exactly a complex series of directions, repeat digit and letter series.	B	Listen carefully and do what I say: "Put this pencil on the floor, open the door, walk around the room, come back, and sit down."		
			M	Listen and repeat these numbers: "2-3, 5-1-8, 4-3-9-6, 7-2-5-1-9."		
			A	Listen carefully and repeat what I say: "School starts in September of each year and Halloween comes in October."		
27.	**Visual Acuity:** The ability to see and to differentiate meaningfully and accurately objects in one's visual field.	Pupil sees without notable fatigue, holds material at appropriate working distance, has no significant loss of acuity on Snellen or Illiterate E chart.	B	Look around this room and tell me all the things you see.		
			M	Look through this cardboard telescope at the picture I am putting up (about 15 feet away) and tell me all about it.		
			A	Now look out the window and name all the things you can see that are as far away as possible.		
28.	**Visual Coordination and Pursuit:** The ability to follow and track objects and symbols with coordinated eye movements.	With head steady, pupil can move eyes to fixate on stable objects in varied places, pursue moving objects such as finger positions, follow picture and word stories left to right without jerky movements.	B	Hold your head straight and move only your eyes. Now look at the door. Look at the ceiling. Look at the floor.		
			M	(Sit in front of pupil with a thumbtack in the eraser of a pencil; hold the pencil about 18 inches from the midline of pupil's nose.) Hold your head still and follow the thumbtack with your eyes as it moves to the left while I count to five. Now follow it to the right while I count to five. Now follow it as it moves up and down while I count to five.		
			A	Hold your head straight; put your right arm straight out in front of you, pointing your thumb up. Now look at what I tell you: "thumb-floor, thumb-window, thumb-table, thumb-ceiling."		

THE PSYCHOEDUCATIONAL INVENTORY OF BASIC LEARNING ABILITIES

Learning Ability	Illustration	Task Level	Specific Learning Task (The examiner should give the following directions to the pupil.)	Notes	Rating Scale VW W A S VS
29. **Visual-Form Discrimination:** The ability to differentiate visually the forms and symbols in one's environment.	Pupil can match identical pictures and symbols such as abstract designs, letters, numbers, and words.	B	(See Workbook for all three tasks.) Look at this picture. Now mark one on this side that looks like the first picture.		
		M	Now look at this picture and mark one on this side that looks like this first picture.		
		A	Look at this picture. Now mark one on this side that looks like the first picture.		
30. **Visual Figure-Ground Differentiation:** The ability to perceive objects in foreground and background and to separate them meaningfully.	Pupil can differentiate picture of self and friends from group picture, differentiate objects in "front" and "back" part of pictures and mock-ups, differentiate his name from among others on paper or chalkboard, perceive simple forms and words imbedded in others.	B	(See Workbook for all three tasks.) Look at this picture. Is the dog in front of the girl? _____ Is the tree behind the girl? _____ Is the wagon behind the tree? _____		
		M	Look at this picture. Find the four hidden figures for me.		
		A	Look at these words. Tell me all the little words you can find in each of these big words.		
31. **Visual Memory:** The ability to recall accurately prior visual experiences.	Pupil can recall from visual cues where he stopped in book, can match or verbally recall objects removed or changed in the environment, can match briefly exposed symbols.	B	(See Workbook for all three tasks.) Look carefully at these four pictures. (Wait five seconds, then cover). Now tell me what you saw.		
		M	Look at this picture. (Expose #1 only for three seconds, keeping others covered. Then cover #1 and uncover the others.) Now I will cover this picture and I want you to find it among these others.		
		A	Look at the word picture. (Follow same procedure as in 31M.) Now I will cover the picture and I want you to find it among these others.		
32. **Visual-Motor Memory:** The ability to reproduce motorwise prior visual experiences.	Pupil can draw designs and symbols following brief exposure, can reproduce letters, numbers, simple words on demand, can portray prior objects or events through gestures or drawings, can reproduce varied patterns and identify hidden materials.	B	(See Workbook for all three tasks.) Look at this picture. (Expose for ten seconds and cover.) Now draw it here. (Point to space in Workbook.)		
		M	Look at this picture. (Expose for ten seconds and cover.) Now draw it here.		
		A	Look at this picture next. (Expose for ten seconds and cover.) Now draw it here.		

Learning Ability	Illustration	Task Level	Specific Learning Task (The examiner should give the following directions to the pupil.)	Notes	Rating Scale VW W A S VS
33. **Visual-Motor Fine Muscle Coordination:** The ability to coordinate fine muscles such as those required in eye-hand tasks.	Pupil can write legibly, trace, and imitate precise body movements without difficulty, can cut, can manipulate, and can judge fine physical responses without gross errors.	B	Untie your shoelaces. Now tie them for me.		
		M	Print or write your whole name for me (see Workbook).		
		A	Look at this picture (see Workbook) and then draw one just like it in the empty box.		
34. **Visual-Motor Spatial-Form Manipulation:** The ability to move in space and to manipulate three-dimensional materials.	Pupil can build block houses and designs, can draw three-dimensional pictures, complete shop and craft projects, integrate form and space puzzles.	B	(See Workbook for all three tasks.) Look at this picture of a book on a table with a pencil across the top. Take this pencil and book and fix them like the picture.		
		M	Look at this picture of the six coins with a pencil across them. Take these coins and this pencil and fix them like the picture.		
		A	Here is a picture of a paper airplane. You copy me, and we will make one together.		
35. **Visual-Motor Speed of Learning:** The ability to learn visual-motor skills from repetitive experience.	Pupil can respond with increasing speed to rote learning tasks such as copying digit or letter sequences, spelling, specific arithmetic processes, and gross motor skills such as jumping over a rope.	B	In the space provided (see Workbook), make as many marks like this (X O +) in that order, as quickly as you can, until I tell you to stop. (Allow 60 seconds.)	Number:	
		M	Take these bolts, washers, and nuts. Put a washer and nut on each bolt like this (demonstrate) as fast as you can. (Use three half-inch bolts, washers, and nuts.)	Time:	
		A	Look at these boxes (see Workbook). Each number has a letter. Look at the numbers and write in the letters that go in the boxes. When you have finished, tell me what it says.	Time:	
36. **Visual-Motor Integration:** The ability to integrate total visual-motor skills in complex problem solving.	Pupil can play complex team sports, swim, draw accurate pictures including people, may play musical instrument, write extended letters, move freely about neighborhood and community.	B	(See Workbook for all three tasks.) Draw a picture of your family.		
		M	Look at this first picture. Now mark each of the following boxes that has a part of the design in the first picture. (Demonstrate by marking first box.)		
		A	Complete the sentence; then copy it on the lines provided.		

THE PSYCHOEDUCATIONAL INVENTORY OF BASIC LEARNING ABILITIES 71

Learning Ability	Illustration	Task Level	Specific Learning Task (The examiner should give the following directions to the pupil.)	Notes	Rating Scale VW W A S VS
LANGUAGE DEVELOPMENT: The current functional stage of total psycho-linguistic development. (Basic learning abilities 37-43)					
37. **Vocabulary:** The ability to understand words.	Pupil has a basic receptive vocabulary in accord with chronological age and educational opportunity.	B	(See Workbook for all three tasks.) Point to the house (woman, rocket, telephone) for me.		
		M	Point to the helmet (skull, juggler, planet) for me.		
		A	Tell me the names of these objects. (Point to kangaroo, television, motorcycle, telescope, stethoscope.)		
38. **Fluency and Encoding:** The ability to express oneself verbally.	Pupil can communicate verbally, has average fluency of speech without undue hesitation or stuttering, uses coherent sentence structure.	B	Listen carefully and then repeat after me: "Georgie Porgie, pudding 'n pie, kissed the girls and made them cry."		
		M	Tell me all of the things you would like to have for your birthday or for Christmas.		
		A	Describe to me in detail what you would like to do next summer during your vacation.		
39. **Articulation:** The ability to articulate words clearly without notable pronunciation or articulatory problems.	Pupil uses words with correct pronunciation of initial, medial, and final sounds.	B	Repeat after me: "brother," "girl," "snake," "chair," "sled," "train," "rate," "blush."		
		M	Good! Now repeat these words: "yellow," "anything," "spring," "fresh," "music," "twins," "drum."		
		A	Now repeat this: "Rub-a-dub-dub, three men in a tub! And who do you think they be?"		
40. **Word Attack Skills:** The ability to analyze words phonetically.	Pupil can make proper phonetic associations, break down words phonetically, recognize component words.	B	(See Workbook for all three tasks.) Look at these words. Now draw a circle around those words that begin with the sound "ch." Now circle those words that begin with "fl."		
		M	Look at all these words again. Draw a line under all the little words you can find that are part of a bigger word. (Demonstrate using the word "beep.")		
		A	Look how the word "band" is created when you add "b" to "and." Now make four other words by adding different letters to "and."		

Learning Ability	Illustration	Task Level	Specific Learning Task (The examiner should give the following directions to the pupil.)	Notes	Rating Scale vW W A S vS
41. **Reading Comprehension:** The ability to understand what one has read.	Pupil can recall story and paraphrase plot, can explain or relate meaningfulness of what has been read.	B	(See Workbook for all three tasks.) Read this sentence and do what it says.		
		M	Read this sentence to yourself. Now tell me what the snake's name is. What is the turtle's name?		
		A	Now read this story aloud. Tell me who this story is about. What did he do in the winter? What happened when he awoke?		
42. **Writing:** The ability to express oneself through written language.	Pupil can write simple sentences and communicate ideas through paragraph, letter, story, or essay.	B	(See Workbook for all three tasks.) Write your name here. Now copy these two words.		
		M	Copy this sentence.		
		A	Now write this sentence: "The old man caught a big fish."		
43. **Spelling:** The ability to spell in both oral and written form.	Pupil spells within general age expectancy.		Tell me how you spell these words: "in"_____ "man"_____ "boy"_____ "house"_____ "person"_____ "Christmas"_____		
		M	Now write these words for me: "go," "girl," "arm," "watch," "circle," "picnic," "airplane."		
		A	Now write this sentence for me: "The jet airplane circled in the sky."		

CONCEPTUAL SKILLS: The functional level of concept attainment and general reasoning ability. (Basic learning abilities 44-49)

Learning Ability	Illustration	Task Level	Specific Learning Task	Notes	Rating Scale
44. **Number Concepts:** The ability to count and use simple numbers to represent quantity.	Pupil can count forward and backward to 100, count by twos, group simple quantities upon request.	B	(See Workbook for all three tasks.) Look at these pictures. Put your finger on the picture with the most pumpkins. Now put your finger on the picture with the least number of cats.		
		M	How many pumpkins are there all together?_____ How many cats are there all together?_____		
		A	How many different groups of things are there?_____ How many different sets of things are there?_____		

THE PSYCHOEDUCATIONAL INVENTORY OF BASIC LEARNING ABILITIES

Learning Ability	Illustration	Task Level	Specific Learning Task (The examiner should give the following directions to the pupil.)	Notes	Rating Scale VW W A S VS
45. **Arithmetic Processes:** The ability to add, subtract, multiply, and divide.	Pupil can demonstrate knowledge of basic processes within expectation of his chronological age.	+	(See Workbook for all four tasks.) Do these addition problems for me. (Ans: 5, 10, 17, 52)		
		−	Good! Now do these subtraction problems. (Ans: 4, 4, 7, 64)		
		×	Very good! Now do these easy multiplication problems. (Ans: 16, 72, 477, 345)		
		÷	Fine! Now do these division problems for me. (Ans: 2, 3, 11, 13)		
46. **Arithmetic Reasoning:** The ability to apply basic arithmetic processes in personal and social usage of problem solving.	Pupil can purchase goods and account for funds, knows coinage and exchange, can calculate time differentials, understands weights and measures.	B	(See Workbook for all three tasks. Read problems orally and have pupil follow in Workbook.)		
			At 4¢ each what would two pencils cost? (Ans: 8¢)		
			Bill receives 60¢ allowance every Friday night. If he saved his money for three weeks, how much would he have altogether? (Ans: $1.80)		
		M	If Joe played football for one and three-quarters hours, how many minutes did he play altogether? (Ans: 105)		
			If one-quarter of a pound of butter costs 21¢, how much would you have to pay for one pound? (Ans: 84¢)		
		A	How many quarts are there in two and one-half gallons of ice cream? (Ans: 10)		
			If eight-inch bricks are used to build a curb line four yards long, how many bricks will be needed. (Ans: 18)		
47. **General Information:** The ability to acquire and utilize general information from education and experience.	Pupil is aware of major local and national current events, knows local geography, has concept of city, state, and nation.	B	What is the name of your closest grocery store? Tell me how to get there.		
		M	Tell me what you know about the country of South Viet Nam.		
		A	Explain to me what a city council does.		
48. **Classification:** The ability to recognize class identities and to use them in establishing logical relationships.	Pupil can sort objects by classification, recognize subclasses, verbalize common elements in class identity.	B	(See Workbook for all three tasks.) Look at these pictures and put a circle around the object that is the smallest in real life. Now draw lines under the two objects that are bigger in real life than the others.		
		M	Now put an X on all those objects that have a similar function or purpose. What is that purpose?		
		A	To what classification would these objects belong? dog _____ man _____ ice cream _____ flower _____		

Learning Ability	Illustration	Task Level	Specific Learning Task (The examiner should give the following directions to the pupil.)	Notes	Rating Scale VW W A S VS
49. **Comprehension:** The ability to use judgment and reasoning in common sense situations.	Pupil responds to factual reasoning when situation is explained to him. He can recognize alternatives in situations and can judge actions accordingly. Pupil can identify logical reasons for given actions.	B	If a house were to catch fire, what do you think might happen?		
		M	What happens to rivers in the spring of the year? Why?		
		A	Explain to me how baseball is played. What are some of the rules of the game?		

SOCIAL SKILLS: The skills involved in social problem solving. (Basic learning abilities 50-53)

50. **Social Acceptance:** The ability to get along with one's peers.	Pupil can relate meaningfully to others and is accepted in both one-to-one and group situations.	B	Do you have friends? Tell me some of their names.		
		M	Tell me how you play with other children before and after school, during recess, and on weekends. Do you belong to any clubs, gangs, groups, or organizations?		
		A	What are good manners? When and how should you use them?		
51. **Anticipatory Response:** The ability to anticipate the probable outcome of a social situation by logical inference.	Pupil can predict the consequences of his own behavior and that of others in given situations.	B	What may happen to a child who runs into the street?		
		M	George always takes his arithmetic homework home with him, but he hardly ever does it. What do you think might happen to him?		
		A	Tell me some of the things you think might happen to boys and girls who get married too young.		
52. **Value Judgments:** The ability to recognize and respond to moral and ethical issues.	Pupil has a sense of right and wrong, controls own actions, demonstrates proper behavior.	B	Diane found a five-dollar bill on the floor near the classroom door. What should she do with it?		
		M	What do you believe is the most important thing in the world?		
		A	What does "justice" mean to you?		
53. **Social Maturity:** The ability to assume personal and social responsibility.	Pupil is socially mature and independent, demonstrates appropriate citizenship, and assumes social responsibility.	B	Do you think children should have certain chores to do or should be expected to help around the house in some way? Why? What kind of chores?		
		M	Tom was riding his bicycle when he saw two men carrying guns and wearing masks going in the front door of a store. What should he do?		
		A	What do you think are some of the responsibilities of a good citizen?		

A PSYCHOEDUCATIONAL EVALUATION OF BASIC LEARNING ABILITIES

Name_____
Date_____Age_____
Evaluator_____

	Performance Level	Learning Disabilities			Learning Strengths	
		Very Weak	Weak	Average	Strong	Very Strong
		0 5	25		75	95 100
GROSS MOTOR DEVELOPMENT						
ROLLING (controlled)						
SITTING (erect)						
CRAWLING (smoothly)						
WALKING (coordinated)						
RUNNING (course)						
THROWING (accurately)						
JUMPING (obstacles)						
SKIPPING (alternately)						
DANCING (eurythmy)						
SELF-IDENTIFICATION (name/awareness)						
BODY LOCALIZATION (part location)						
BODY ABSTRACTION (transfer/generalization)						
MUSCULAR STRENGTH (sit-, leg-ups/bends)						
GENERAL PHYSICAL HEALTH (significant history)						
SENSORY-MOTOR INTEGRATION						
BALANCE AND RHYTHM (games/dance)						
BODY-SPATIAL ORGANIZATION (mazes)						
REACTION-SPEED DEXTERITY (motor-accuracy)						
TACTILE DISCRIMINATION (object identification)						
DIRECTIONALITY (right-left/etc.)						
LATERALITY (hand-eye-foot)						
TIME ORIENTATION (lapse and concept)						
PERCEPTUAL-MOTOR SKILLS						
AUDITORY: ACUITY (functional hearing)						
A—DECODING (following directions)						
A—VOCAL ASSOCIATION (imitative response)						
A—MEMORY (retention)						
A—SEQUENCING (patterning)						
VISUAL: ACUITY ("Snellen")						
V—COORDINATION AND PURSUIT (tracking)						
V—FORM DISCRIMINATION (association)						
V—FIGURE/GROUND (differentiation)						
V—MEMORY (visual recall)						

A PSYCHOEDUCATIONAL EVALUATION OF BASIC LEARNING ABILITIES (Continued)

	Performance Level	Learning Disabilities			Learning Strengths	
		Very Weak	Weak	Average	Strong	Very Strong
		0 5	25		75	95 100
VISUAL-MOTOR: MEMORY *(designs)*						
VM—FINE MUSCLE COORDINATION *(designs)*						
VM—SPATIAL-FORM MANIPULATION *(blocks)*						
VM—SPEED OF LEARNING *(coding)*						
VM—INTEGRATION *(draw-a-man)*						
LANGUAGE DEVELOPMENT						
VOCABULARY *(word knowledge)*						
FLUENCY AND ENCODING *(use and structure)*						
ARTICULATION *(initial/medial/final)*						
WORD ATTACK SKILLS *(phonic association)*						
READING COMPREHENSION *(understanding)*						
WRITING *(expression)*						
SPELLING *(oral/written)*						
CONCEPTUAL SKILLS						
NUMBER CONCEPTS *(counting)*						
ARITHMETIC PROCESSES *(+ − × ÷)*						
ARITHMETIC REASONING *(problem solving)*						
GENERAL INFORMATION *(fund of knowledge)*						
CLASSIFICATION *(relationships)*						
COMPREHENSION *(common sense reasoning)*						
SOCIAL SKILLS						
SOCIAL ACCEPTANCE *(friendship)*						
ANTICIPATORY RESPONSE *(foresight)*						
VALUE JUDGMENTS *(ethical-moral sense)*						
SOCIAL MATURITY *(gross problem solving)*						

SAMPLE Reduced in Size

STUDENT WORKBOOK

Copyright © MCMLXVIII by Lear Siegler, Inc./Fearon Publishers, 6 Davis Drive, Belmont California 94002. All rights reserved. No part of this book may be reproduced by any means, nor transmitted, nor translated into a machine language, without written permission from the publisher.

78   LEARNING DISABILITIES

10 A (3 NAMES)

12 B	12 M
16 B	17 B

20 B (FIRST NAME)

23 B

23 A

8   5   1

THE PSYCHOEDUCATIONAL INVENTORY OF BASIC LEARNING ABILITIES

29 B | **D** | D | O | D | D | Ɛ

29 M | (5 dots) | (4 dots) | (4 dots) | (5 dots) | (6 dots) | (4 dots)

29 A | **then** | than | them | tben | ther | then

30 B / 30 M

30 A | ILLINOIS | THANKSGIVING | WASHINGTON

80   LEARNING DISABILITIES

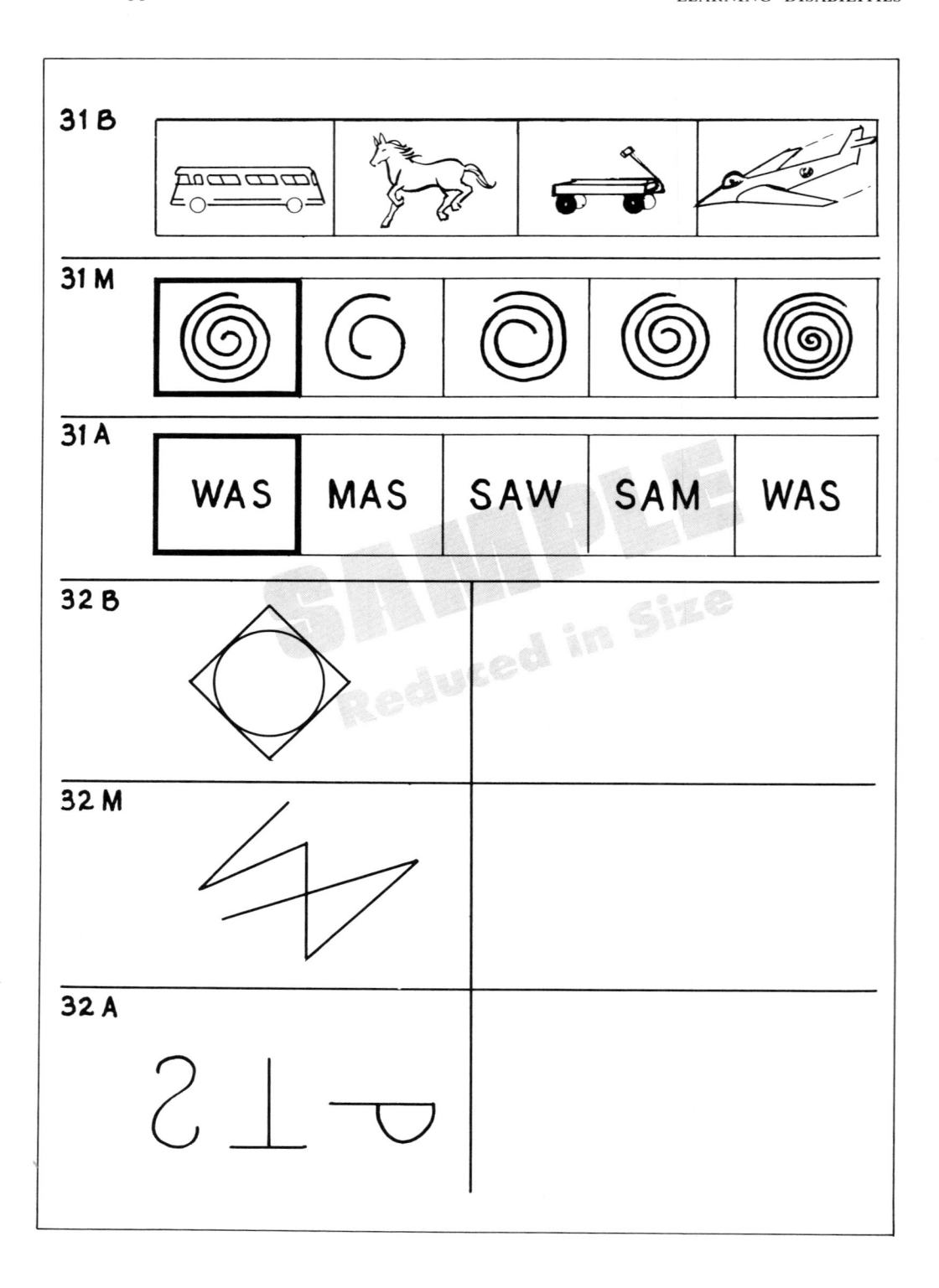

31 B

31 M

31 A | **WAS** | MAS | SAW | SAM | WAS |

32 B

32 M

32 A

SAMPLE Reduced in Size

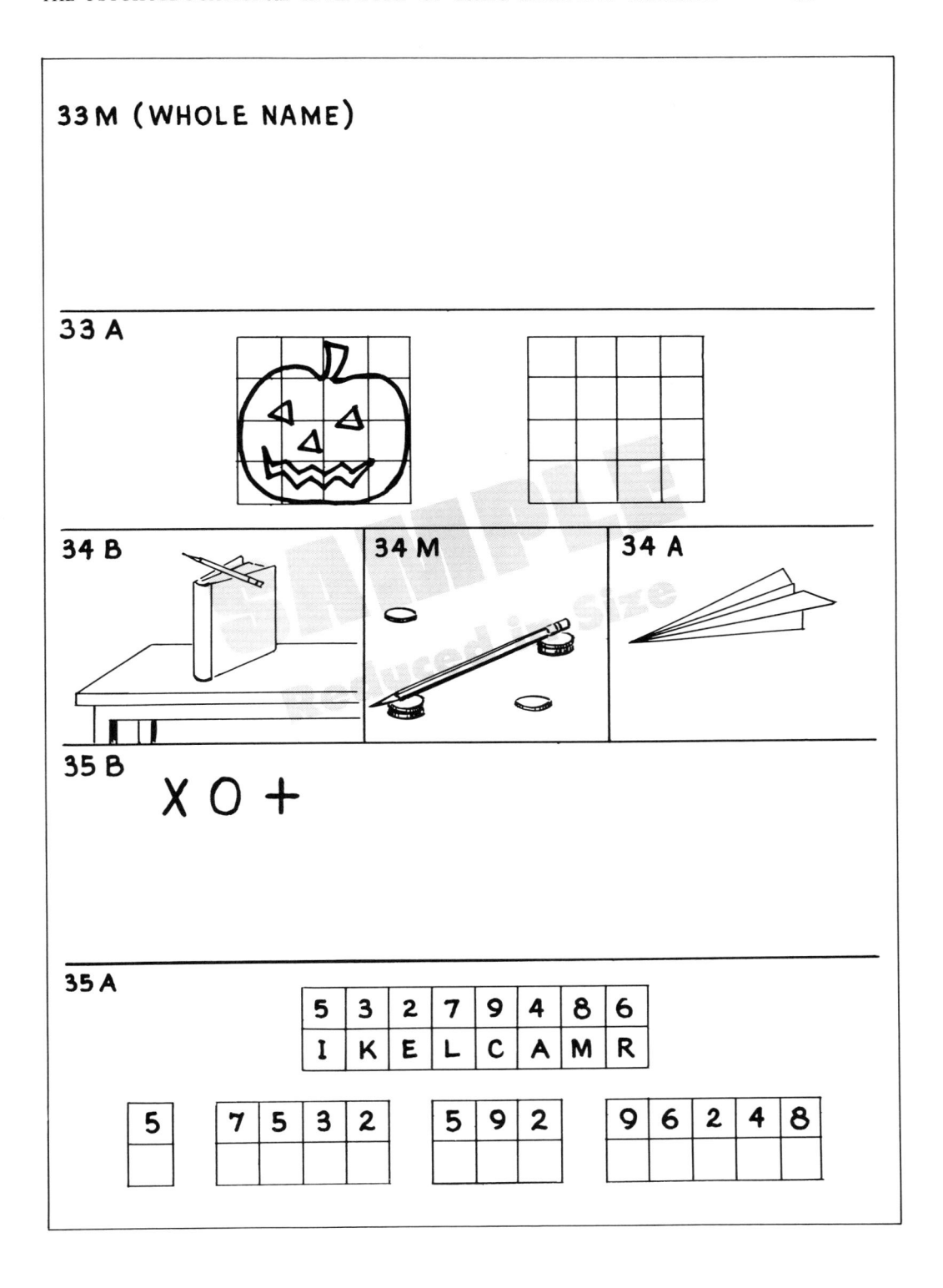

THE PSYCHOEDUCATIONAL INVENTORY OF BASIC LEARNING ABILITIES   81

33 M (WHOLE NAME)

33 A

34 B   **34 M**   **34 A**

35 B   X O +

35 A

5	3	2	7	9	4	8	6
I	K	E	L	C	A	M	R

5

7	5	3	2

5	9	2

9	6	2	4	8

82 LEARNING DISABILITIES

36 B (FAMILY)

36 M

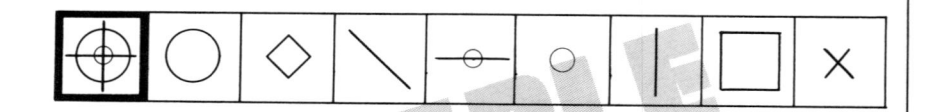

36 A *The food I like to eat best of all is* _____.

37 B, M

37 A

40 B, M

CHURCH   FLEE   SLEEP   SOMETHING

BEEP   CRAWL   THOSE   CHAIR   GREAT

EVERYWHERE   FLY   TOMORROW

40 A

BAND   __AND   __AND   __AND   __AND

41 B

Draw a circle around the box.

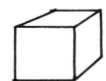

41 M

The snake's name is Sam and the turtle's name is Mary.

84 LEARNING DISABILITIES

41 A During the cold winter the bear cub stayed in the cave and slept. When he awoke, the flowers were blooming and the grass was turning green. Then he was hungry so he began to look for food. He wished he could find some honey to eat.

42 B

NAME AND ADDRESS

Candy ——————— *birthday*

42 M

Pumpkins smile on Halloween.

42 A

43 M

43 A

44 B, M, A

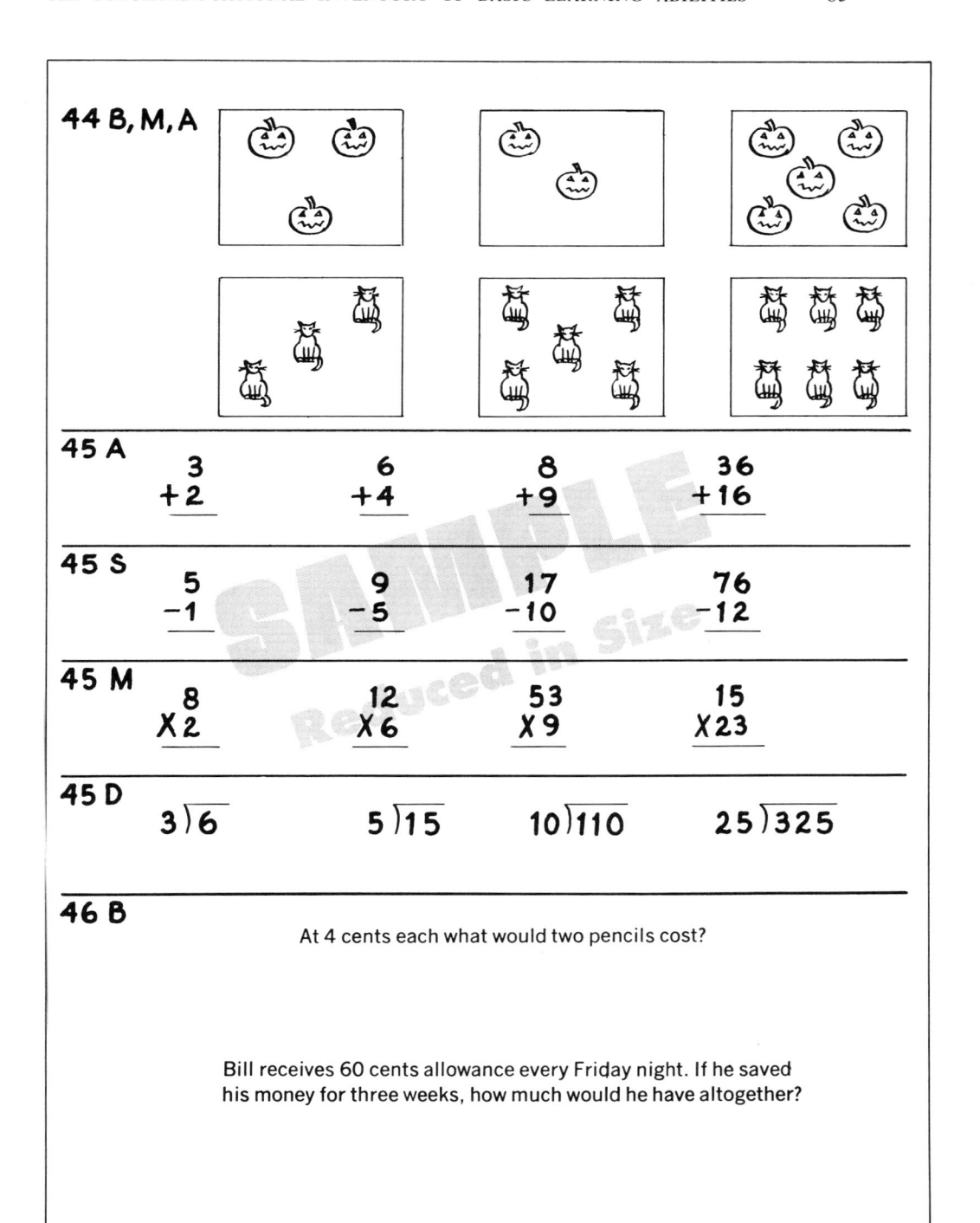

45 A

```
    3          6          8         36
   +2         +4         +9        +16
  ___        ___        ___       ___
```

45 S

```
    5          9         17         76
   -1         -5        -10        -12
  ___        ___        ___       ___
```

45 M

```
    8         12         53         15
   ×2         ×6         ×9        ×23
  ___        ___        ___       ___
```

45 D

3)6   5)15   10)110   25)325

46 B

At 4 cents each what would two pencils cost?

Bill receives 60 cents allowance every Friday night. If he saved his money for three weeks, how much would he have altogether?

46 M If Joe played football for one and three-quarters hours, how many minutes did he play altogether?

If one-quarter of a pound of butter costs 21 cents, how much would you have to pay for one pound?

46 A How many quarts are there in two and one-half gallons of ice cream?

If eight-inch-long bricks are used to build a curb line four yards long, how many bricks will be needed?

48 B, M, A

CHAPTER 8
Self-evaluation devices

As was stressed in Chapter 1, the third step in the diagnostic-prescriptive process is pupil self-assessment and involvement. Without self-assessment and early involvement in the determination of his own behavior, the child may become alienated from the educational setting in which he finds himself. A common subsequent result is a lack of motivation, which is usually quite difficult to counteract. Searching immediately for pupil interests and self-perceived strengths often makes it possible to use these insights in the development of a meaningful educational program.

There are many ways by which pupils can be involved in their own self-evaluation. Perhaps the most common is to engage the child in a series of ongoing conversations in which he has the opportunity to relate his self-concepts and to discuss his concerns. Various kinds of checklists, tests, and inventories may also help in pinpointing critical self-perceptions, abilities, and interests. A simple and frequently used approach is to present the pupil with a form similar to the self-evaluation check sheet in Figure 9, which provides him with the opportunity to indicate his concerns briefly. Most teachers can devise such check sheets so that they are appropriate for the developmental level and distinctive characteristics of the class or group with which they are working. The essential components of a good check sheet are (1) open-ended questions that permit the individual to respond freely and (2) the chance for the pupil to rate himself in the usual subject matter areas of general concern. What is being obtained from such a check sheet is a number of self-perceptions, the validity of which needs to be determined by the teacher through systematic observation and through the evaluation of corresponding data from other sources.

AFFECTIVE RE-EDUCATION

Another kind of self-evaluation is a systematic self-analysis of problem behavior. Diagnostic-prescriptive teachers and therapists who work with children who have significant behavior disorders often spend much time in attempting to help them develop personal insights and positive goal orientations. The diagnostic-prescriptive teacher thus becomes a guidance person who helps the pupil to consider and explore his problem and to think rationally; further, through individual and group discussion and counseling, he helps him to change his behavior. Essentially, this process is emotional or affective *re*-education, since old habits and behaviors are re-examined, "unlearned," and replaced by more personally desirable ones. Although there are many forms of re-education, all of them demand the development of self-awareness, insight, recognition of alternative actions, self-determination, and personal and social reinforcement.

A SELF-EVALUATION CHECK SHEET

My name is_____ My birthday is_____

The day today is_____

I am really interested in_____
_____

I enjoy_____
_____

I have trouble with_____
_____

What I want to learn next is_____
_____

My strengths are_____
_____

I need help in_____
_____

My hobbies are_____
_____

If I had my way,_____
_____

I know most about_____
_____

I feel_____
_____

Figure 9.

SELF-EVALUATION DEVICES

Check ( ) the boxes below to show how well you do in each subject

	I do very well in this subject	I do OK in this subject	I do not do well in this subject	I have a lot of trouble in this subject
Writing				
Spelling				
Mathematics				
Science				
Reading				
Art				
Music				
Social Science				
Physical Education				
Speaking				

The subjects I like the most are _____

Figure 9. (continued)

For older elementary school pupils and for secondary school students, the self-evaluation and behavior change questionnaire that follows is recommended.

Step 1: Personal Problem Behavior. Describe the behavior that you are most concerned about.

Step 2: Possible Causes. Explain what might have caused this behavior.

Step 3: Self-judgment. Describe how *you* feel and what you believe about your behavior.

Step 4: Social Judgment. Describe what your parents, friends, relatives, and other people believe or feel about your behavior.

Step 5: Irrational Attitudes. Try to identify and describe some of the irrational or illogical beliefs and feelings you have about your problem.

Step 6: Positive Alternatives. Describe some more positive ways of acting that you might try in dealing with your problem.

Step 7: Personal Aspirations. Select a goal to work toward and explain what you would like to do.

Step 8: Plan. Describe how you can start to work on your goal or aspiration.

Step 9: Personal and Social Consequences. What do you feel might happen to you if you follow the plan?

Step 10: Help. How might others help you with your plan?

Because they are psychologically sound and in a logical sequence that offers a means to gain self-awareness and create a behavior change, these ten steps comprise a workable instrument for self-evaluation. The questionnaire should be presented in a format that allows the student time to reflect and to evaluate himself accordingly. It is used most effectively when it becomes the basis for follow-up discussion and counseling sessions in which the diagnostic-prescriptive teacher and the peer group aid the pupil in the completion of his self-evaluation and in the subsequent consideration of alternative behaviors.

MY GOAL RECORD

A final example of a self-evaluation device is Figure 10. This kind of device is designed to enhance the importance of goal-directed behavior and personal motivation. Prerequisite to its use is the involvement of the pupil in the diagnostic-prescriptive process and his progression to the point where he is eager to select his own specific learning or behavior goals and capable of doing so. The major purposes of this device are to help sharpen the learner's perception of his goal through the selection of highly specific targets for learning, to aid him in determining his own rewards and consequences, and to provide him with a record of his continuous progress toward his goal. As a motivational device, this kind of self-evaluation instrument is especially valuable as part of an ongoing behavior modification program. It may be used with groups or with individual pupils.

SELF-EVALUATION DEVICES 91

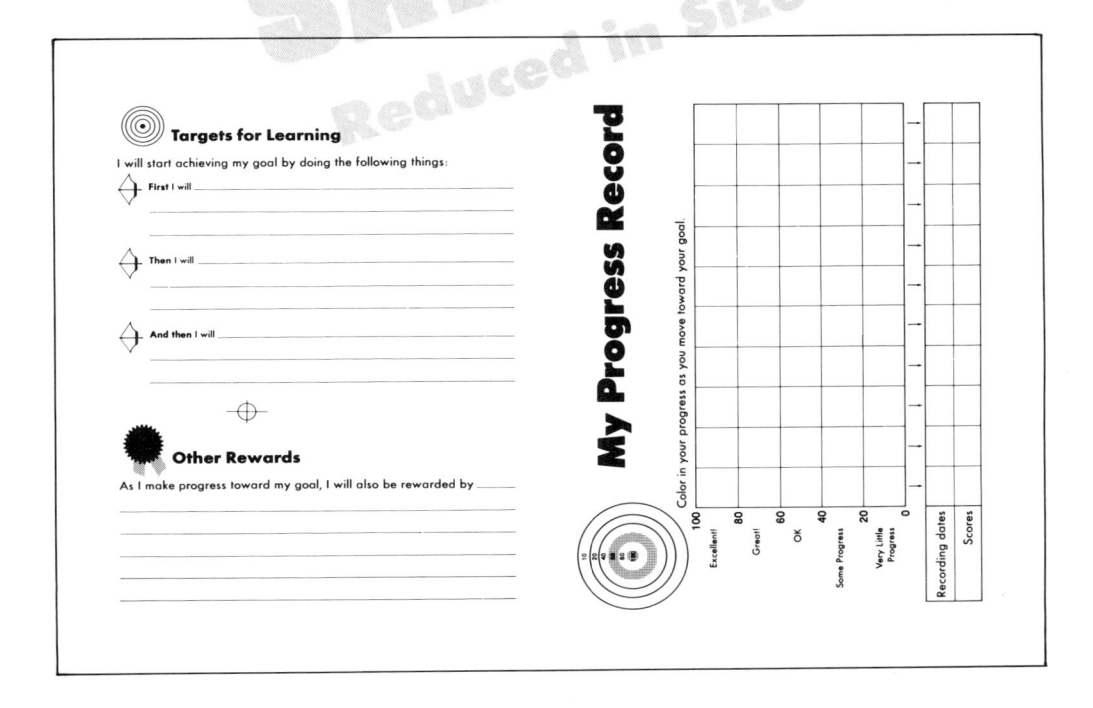

Figure 10.

CHAPTER 9
Specifying priority objectives

The goal of the diagnostic-prescriptive evaluation is to obtain information that can be used in helping the pupil to become a more effective learner. If the data from evaluation instruments fail to suggest what the child needs to learn, they are worthless for prescriptive purposes. One of the major functions of the diagnostic-prescriptive teacher is the analysis of available data to derive teaching strategies. In order to develop prescriptive lessons and determine teaching procedures, learning objectives must be clearly and concisely stated. If the teacher is not absolutely clear as to her learning objectives and the rationale behind them, the chances are that her subsequent efforts will fail to meet the educational needs of the child with learning or behavior difficulties.

It is important to understand that the conclusion of the diagnostic-prescriptive evaluation process is not in the establishment of scores or the assignment of such labels as "mentally retarded" or "perceptually handicapped," but in the derivation of possible learning objectives. A good reading test, for example, should expose areas of difficulty for the learner and suggest some specific reading skills that he should be taught. In a similar fashion, initial screening information from referring teachers, comments and ratings from parents' assessment of their children, and self-evaluation information from the pupil himself should all suggest possible learning objectives. All of the instruments presented in previous chapters contain critical learning tasks that may serve as criteria for the development of prescriptive education programs. By carefully reviewing pupil performance on each task, it is possible to determine whether or not that task should be considered as an objective for prescriptive teaching.

DETERMINING INDIVIDUAL LEARNING OBJECTIVES

The use of the *Determining Individual Learning Objectives* form (Figure 11) has been found helpful by many teachers attempting to derive learning objectives from diagnostic information. This form permits all diagnostic evaluation data to be summarized in terms of its teaching implications. It recognizes a five-step evaluation procedure that includes information from (1) the referring teacher, (2) the parents, (3) the pupil, (4) the diagnostic-prescriptive teacher, and (5) consultants or other sources. In columns under each of these sources of evaluation,

Figure 11.

the name of the instrument or instruments used and the date administered are indicated. Thus, *A Basic Screening and Referral Form for Children with Suspected Learning and Behavioral Disabilities* is listed as the instrument used by the referring teacher, and the *Developmental Task Analysis* is listed as the instrument used by parents in the assessment of their own child. There are several kinds of self-evaluation devices (see Chapter 8), and the one used must be specified. Diagnostic-prescriptive teacher evaluations, which are usually comprehensive, consist of direct observations of behavior, specific task analyses, inventories, and standardized tests. *A Psychoeducational Inventory of Basic Learning Abilities, An Inventory of Primary Skills,* and *The Spache Diagnostic Reading Scales* are recommended as appropriate instruments to be used here. However, according to pupil need and teacher preference, many other instruments are also used; thus, *The Gray Oral Reading Test, the Stanford Achievement Tests, Wide Range Achievement Tests,* and others would also be listed if used. Column 5 provides for input from such consultants as psychologists, physicians, and language specialists; blank spaces are furnished so that the instruments used (Bender, neurological examination, Binet, *Wechsler Intelligence Scale for Children, Illinois Test of Psycholinguistic Ability,* or others) may be written in.

The six developmental learning areas are listed within their educational domains in the column on the far left. Thus, gross motor, sensory-motor, and perceptual-motor learning objectives are placed in the psychomotor domain. The cognitive domain includes language and conceptual learning objectives; and social and personal learning objectives are in the affective domain. As the directions state, the teacher is to review the data obtained from each instrument carefully and then develop one possible learning objective in each appropriate developmental learning area.

For example, upon reviewing *A Basic Screening and Referral Form for Children with Suspected Learning and Behavioral Disabilities* as completed by the referring teacher, it might be decided that the social-personal behavior difficulty of most concern was: Does not accept social responsibility. Accordingly, this could be specified as the major social-personal learning objective derived from referring-teacher evaluation data; it might then be written in the space as:

> For Mary to be able to accept some social responsibility within the class.

From the *Developmental Task Analysis,* Mary's parents might have indicated much concern over her apparent inability to write her ABC's. This could be selected as another objective and written in the language learning objective space as:

> Mary needs to learn to write her ABC's.

Another illustration is from the evaluation data obtained directly by the diagnostic-prescriptive teacher using *A Psychoeducational Inventory of Basic*

Learning Abilities. It might be decided that auditory sequencing is the perceptual skill most in need of development at this time. This could be stated as a learning objective in the following way:

> I want Mary to learn how to listen carefully to a random series of letters and numbers and repeat them correctly.

The same procedure is followed for deriving possible learning objectives from the other sources of evaluation information. However, since some instruments, such as reading and arithmetic tests, do not provide data in all developmental learning areas, these spaces are not used.

When all possible spaces have been filled in, the diagnostic-prescriptive teacher will have compiled approximately thirty-six learning objectives. Obviously, it is neither practicable nor necessary to develop educational programs to accomplish all of these objectives at once; priorities must be established in order for practical planning to occur. This ordering is quickly done by reviewing all possible objectives as written in each developmental learning area and selecting the most important one on which to begin work. For example, a brief survey of the five spaces containing possible social-personal learning objectives might result in specifying that priority be given to teaching Mary "to be able to cooperate with classmates in ten social learning activities each day." A priority objective would also be selected in each of the other five developmental learning areas, and these are then ranked for teacher consideration and educational programming. If such a procedure is followed at least once a year, it is possible to develop meaningful learning objectives and prescriptive-teaching plans from relevant diagnostic procedures.

As soon as priority learning objectives have been selected, the teacher is faced with the problem of devising teaching strategies and developing the educational program in such a way that the objectives may be realized. In order to accomplish this, it is important that the child with learning or behavior difficulties be involved in the determination of his own learning objectives and in the design or selection of his educational program. This involvement becomes possible through discussing with him the probable learning objectives and then helping him specify the priority objective of the moment and some ways in which he can begin to monitor his progress. Two ways of doing this are presented in the remainder of this chapter.

SPECIFIC BEHAVIOR RECORD

The Specific Behavior Record (Figure 12) contains a simple chart that permits the teacher (or pupil) to graph the pupil's progress toward his objective. The basic identifying information appears at the top of the form. In the example, we see that Mary's progress in cooperating with others is being charted. It is assumed here that Mary has been made aware of the desirability of learning to cooperate with others and that the teacher has now begun to develop a program

SPECIFIC BEHAVIOR RECORD

Pupil _Mary T._ Age _7½_ Behavior recorded _cooperating with classmates_

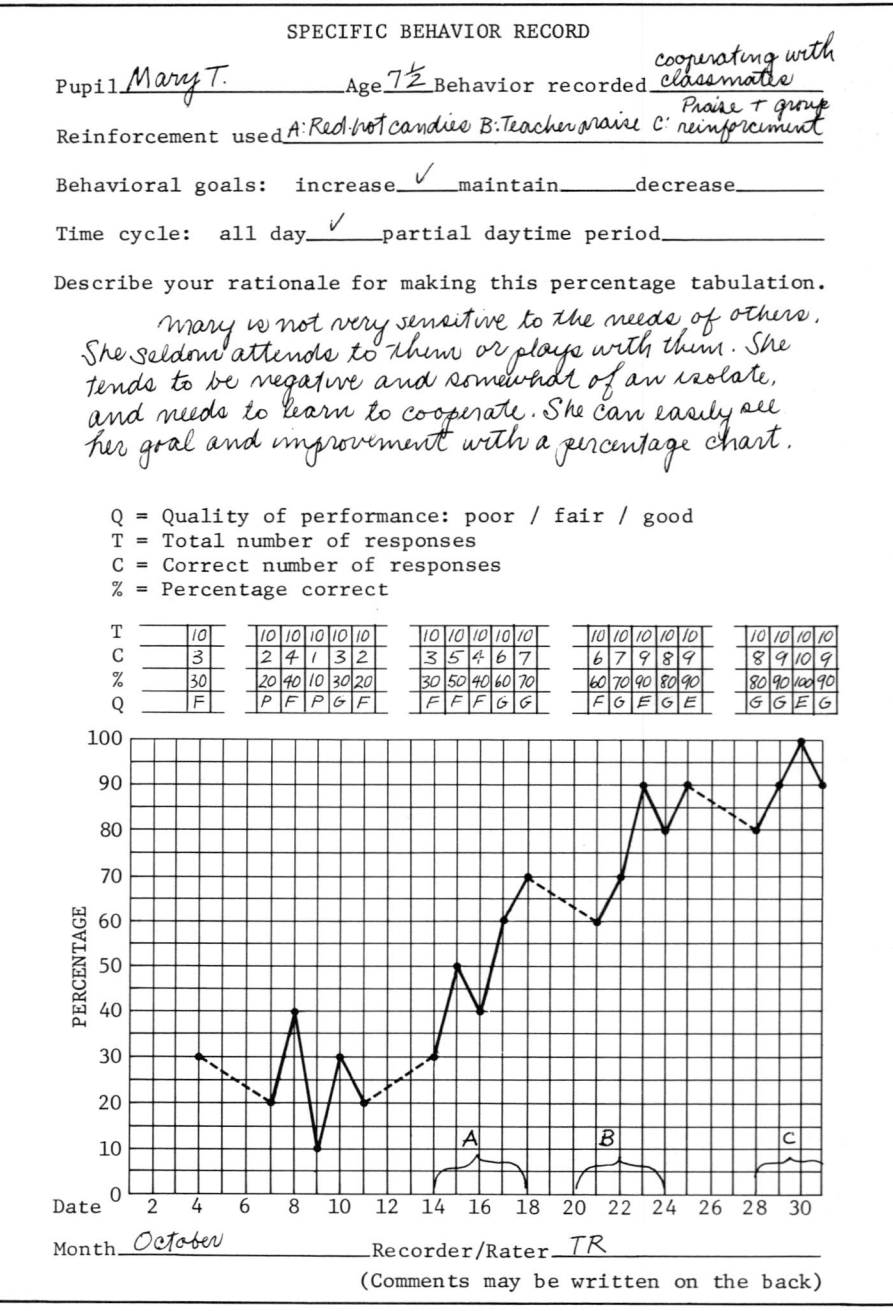

Reinforcement used _A: Red-hot candies B: Teacher praise C: Praise + group reinforcement_

Behavioral goals: increase _✓_ maintain _____ decrease _____

Time cycle: all day _✓_ partial daytime period _____

Describe your rationale for making this percentage tabulation.

Mary is not very sensitive to the needs of others. She seldom attends to them or plays with them. She tends to be negative and somewhat of an isolate, and needs to learn to cooperate. She can easily see her goal and improvement with a percentage chart.

Q = Quality of performance: poor / fair / good
T = Total number of responses
C = Correct number of responses
% = Percentage correct

T	10		10	10	10	10	10		10	10	10	10	10		10	10	10	10	10		10	10	10	10
C	3		2	4	1	3	2		3	5	4	6	7		6	7	9	8	9		8	9	10	9
%	30		20	40	10	30	20		30	50	40	60	70		60	70	90	80	90		80	90	100	90
Q	F		P	F	P	G	F		F	F	F	G	G		F	G	E	G	E		G	G	E	G

Date: 2 4 6 8 10 12 14 16 18 20 22 24 26 28 30

Month _October_   Recorder/Rater _TR_

(Comments may be written on the back)

Figure 12.

SPECIFYING PRIORITY OBJECTIVES

to this end. The prescriptive learning exercises designed for Mary consist of ten daily activities through which she may be guided into developing cooperative behavior; these are:

Recess play time: Two opportunities daily (morning and afternoon) to accept arranged invitations to play from classmates.

Room clean-up team: Two opportunities daily to work with an assigned team of five pupils to erase the chalkboard and straighten chairs.

Game time: One opportunity daily to play with another child during an established time.

Social studies mural team: One opportunity daily to work on a team building a mural.

Physical education—cooperative team play: One opportunity daily to participate in team sports as assigned.

Helping another child: One opportunity daily to help an assigned child in arithmetic or reading.

Lining up at lunch: One opportunity daily to cooperate in establishing order for moving to the cafeteria.

Helping deliver milk: One opportunity daily to help on a team performing a socially useful function.

The Specific Behavior Record shows that the program was started on October 4, with Mary responding positively to three of the ten learning opportunities, thus achieving 30 percent proficiency. Since this is far below a desirable expectancy of 90 to 100 percent cooperation, the quality of her performance was rated by the teacher as "fair." For the first six-day learning period of October (4, 7, 8, 9, 10, 11), the teacher worked to establish the cooperative program. Mary's responses to it were used as a baseline against which to measure her later progress.

During the second full week, October 14 through 18, the teacher introduced "red-hot candies" as an immediate reward. When Mary responded by positive participation in the program, she was presented with five red-hots for each cooperative behavior. These responses were tabulated as reinforcement period "A," and reflect a gradual improvement of achievement to 70 percent on October 18, which was judged by the teacher as "good" performance.

During the week of October 21–25, the teacher began to use praise along with red-hots as reinforcers. When Mary demonstrated cooperative behavior, the teacher immediately went to her and commented on it; occasionally, she patted her on the back as well. Performance continued to improve to 90 percent cooperative behavior on October 23 and 25, and on both these days the quality of her performance was rated "excellent." This period was designated as reinforcement period "B."

SELF-REPORT OF DAILY LEARNING OBJECTIVES

Pupil's name _____   Date _____

Time	Subject	Materials required	Learning objective (when you have completed this lesson you should be able to...)	Self Rating*	Self-evaluation (What mistakes did I make? How can I correct these mistakes?)
1 9:05– 9:40 AM	Reading/phonics word attack	Phonics Is Fun Book III	To pronounce six blends and use them correctly in 24 words.	G (Good; 19 correct)	Mistakes were with "ag" and "gl" blends. Need to practice those words missed and others ones.
2					
3					
4					
5					

*Self Rating: E–excellent (90–100 per cent correct). G–good (75–90 per cent correct). A–average (25–75 per cent correct). F–fair (10–25 per cent correct). P–poor (1–10 per cent correct).

Figure 13.

On October 28, the teacher dropped the candy reinforcement for Mary, but continued teacher praise. In addition, a token system, which required Mary to record her own progress on the chart with the aid of her teammates, was established. For each day that her chart showed 90 or 100 percent cooperation, Mary and the other four children on her team were rewarded with extra dessert from the cafeteria at lunch the following day. This constituted reinforcement period "C," and the chart reflects the continued improvement in cooperative behavior.

Such a procedure illustrates one way in which priority learning objectives may be specified and used as the basis for developing a prescriptive program. Behavior records such as these are extremely helpful to both teacher and child in determining progress toward stated objectives and in determining the effects of prescriptive innovations and interventions. There are numerous other ways to record progress toward prescriptive goals and objectives; several of these are presented in *Effective Teaching: A Guide to Diagnostic-Prescriptive Task Analysis,*[*] which should be referred to by those interested in learning about such matters in more detail.

SELF-REPORT OF DAILY LEARNING OBJECTIVES

Another way of making specified learning objectives relevant to the prescriptive educational program is to provide a summary sheet for self-reporting of progress made. The model presented in Figure 13 is representative of the many possible approaches to self-reporting of pupil progress. This particular example portrays *daily* learning objectives, but the same procedure can be used for recording progress toward learning objectives spanning several days or weeks.

After the pupil's name and the date, the time of day is specified. That is followed by the subject area and the material required in the lesson. The learning objective is then written out in precise terms. As children accommodate themselves to prescriptive procedures, they should be guided in arranging their own daily learning schedules and in selecting and writing the objectives for their lessons. Following completion of the lesson, the pupil rates himself on a scale from poor to excellent. The final entry is a student notation of the kinds of mistakes made and comments as to how these might be corrected.

This kind of recording device serves several purposes: it helps the teacher in planning learning activities directly related to the specified priority objectives, it enables the pupil to become more self-aware and self-determinant through involvement in rating his own performance, and it provides a means of recording progress, therefore contributing to the ongoing evaluation and modification of individual learning objectives.

---

[*]Robert E. Valett, *Effective Teaching: A Guide to Diagnostic-Prescriptive Task Analysis* (Belmont, Calif.: Fearon Publishers, 1970).

SUMMARY

In this chapter, three means of specifying priority learning objectives have been presented. The first was concerned with the derivation of possible learning objectives from available diagnostic information. The second illustrated the pinpointing and charting of a single behavioral objective. The third illustrated how the pupil may be involved in the specification and ongoing evaluation of daily learning objectives. Modification of all of these means should be made to suit the distinctive needs of the diagnostic-prescriptive teacher and her pupils.

PART 3

CASE STUDIES AND APPLICATIONS

Several case studies are presented in the third part of this book to illustrate the use of the instruments and procedures presented in Part 2. Naturally, the real names of the children are not those used. The case reports are otherwise unaltered as to fact or interpretation; they have been corrected and edited only for spelling, arrangement, and like matters. These examples demonstrate various approaches to the use of diagnostic-prescriptive instruments. Jay, Mitch, Robbie, and T. W. (Chapters 10–13) were all evaluated by single teachers. Peri (Chapter 14) was the subject of a unique team approach to diagnostic-prescriptive intervention. The case of Beverly T. (Chapter 16) shows how the learning-resource model may be put into effect. Chapter 17 discusses problems in the use of I.Q. tests and scores in the prescriptive teaching of children such as Billy J.

CHAPTER 10
Using task analysis with intelligence testing: Jay

Jay is an educationally handicapped child aged eight years. He is in a regular class and receives supplemental help from a resource teacher. The learning-disability teacher who conducted this evaluation, the author of this chapter, is Aileen Elliott. This case illustrates how traditional standardized-test information *(Wechsler Intelligence Scale for Children, Illinois Test of Psycholinguistic Ability,* and the like) can be used along with task analysis instruments to develop a prescriptive program. In this situation, Jay was seen daily for a scheduled period of time in the school's learning-disability room. He received prescriptive teaching and educational therapy there; then he returned to the regular class for the remainder of the day.

BACKGROUND INFORMATION

Jay, age eight years, is Mexican-American, the fifth of six children whose ages range from fourteen years to eighteen months. Their attitude toward him is one of indifference except in the case of the eighteen-month-old brother, who dislikes Jay, will not allow Jay to touch him, does not want to be close to him.

His gestation period and birth were normal, although the mother thinks it may have been a breech birth. His developmental history up to age five is sketchy. The mother does not remember at what age he said his first word or first sentence, although she was pretty sure that he rolled over at four months, sat alone at five, crawled at eight or nine months, and walked at fourteen months.

At age four he fell from an upper bunk onto the cement floor. He did not lose consciousness, and no doctor was consulted. At age six, he again hit his head as a result of a fall. There was a small cut and lots of blood. Again, no doctor was consulted.

Jay is subject to allergic rhinitis, medication for which makes him sleepy. He yawns frequently during the first hour of the school day.

TESTS GIVEN BY THE PSYCHOLOGIST

All put him in the normal range.

Peabody Vocabulary. 92 I.Q. (receptive vocabulary; four pictures shown; the examiner says "man" and the child points).
Goodenough Draw-a-man. 100 I.Q. (tests cognitive and motor skills).
Wechsler Intelligence Scale for Children. Full scale 92; verbal, 91; performance, 94.
Wide Range Achievement Test.

Subject	Grade	Standard Score	Percent
Reading	K.3	66	1
Spelling	1.2	78	7
Arithmetic	1.2	78	7

TESTS GIVEN IN THE LEARNING DISABILITY GROUP

Jay entered the Learning Disability Group when he was age eight years five months.

Frostig Developmental Test of Visual Perception.
Kephart Perceptual-motor Survey.
Illinois Test of Psycholinguistic Ability (auditory and visual understanding).
Valett's *Psychoeducational Inventory of Basic Learning Abilities.*
Durrell's *Analysis of Reading Difficulty.*

STRENGTHS FOUND BY THE TESTING

Wechsler Intelligence Scale for Children

1. *Comprehension* (scaled score 14), which tests judgment, understanding, and common sense in practical situations. It requires that the child draw upon past experiences in solving common-sense problems and situations. (Example: What should you do if you cut your finger?)
2. *Picture arrangement* (scaled score 12), which measures the ability to see a total situation and foresee results. It is based on comprehension, organization, and environmental experiences. (Example: Four pictures of a burglar to sequence.)
3. *Block design* (scaled score 11), which measures the ability to perceive, analyze, synthesize, and reproduce abstract designs using nonverbal concept formation. It measures the capacity for sustained effort, visual-motor coordination, abstract and concrete thinking ability. (Example: Blocks are used to produce a pattern from a two-dimensional picture. The blocks are similar to the *Try Task Blocks.*)

Illinois Test of Psycholinguistic Ability

ITPA found him to be stronger in visual than in auditory areas.

1. *Gestures*—age 10.4 plus.
2. *Visual association*—age 9.4, classifying and categorizing at a visual level. (Example: The child sees a picture of a hammer, and chooses from a pin, needle, nail, and knife.)
3. *Visual closure*—age 10.6 plus (recognizing a picture on seeing a part of it. (Example: The fin of a fish.)
4. *Auditory sequencing*—age 10.3 plus. (He could repeat a series of six numbers.)

Valett's *Psychoeducational Inventory of Basic Learning Abilities*

1. *Auditory acuity*—Jay could repeat or follow simple instructions whispered behind his back or spoken *very* softly from a distance of twenty feet.
2. *Auditory sequencing*—repeating a series of six numbers.

WEAKNESSES FOUND BY THE TESTING

Wechsler Intelligence Scale for Children

1. *Object assembly* was the lowest (scaled score 6). Measures visual-motor coordination, simple assembly skills, the ability to use spatial relationships, and the ability to synthesize concrete parts into meaningful wholes. (Example: To assemble the parts of a face.)
2. *Information* (scaled score 7). Measures associative thinking and general comprehension of facts which are acquired both in the home and in the school. The acquisition is based on the child's interest, background, alertness to his surroundings, and to his overall urge to collect knowledge. (Example: What animal gives milk? What do we do to make water boil?)
3. *Arithmetic* (scaled score 7). Measures attention and mental concentration, uses abstract concepts of numbers. (Example: If I cut an apple in half, how many pieces will I have?)
4. *Similarities* (scaled score 7). Tests remote auditory memory, abstract and concrete reasoning abilities. Involves verbal concept formation and the capacity for associative thinking. (Example: How are cat and mouse alike? "They are both animals" is a better answer than "They both have tails.")
5. *Vocabulary* (scaled score 8). Measures the child's ability to understand words and reflects his level of education and environment. This is an abstract ability and has no relation to reading ability. (Example: "Cushion is to sit on" is not as good an answer as "pillow.")
6. *Picture completion* (scaled score 8). Measures the ability to visualize essential from nonessential detail and to identify familiar stimuli from one's environment. (Examples: A picture of a comb with two teeth missing; a rooster with a spur missing, and the child must say "spur.")

Illinois Test of Psycholinguistic Ability

A. Auditory Areas

1. *Auditory reception,* age 4.5. His first miss was on "Do ants crawl?"
2. *Auditory association,* age 5.3. First miss was on "Coffee is bitter, sugar is _____."
3. *Grammatic closure,* age 5.10. (Example: Mother is opening the can. Here is the can she _____ (open).) Jay said "mans" for "men," "muchest" for "most," "foots" for "feet."
4. *Auditory closure,* age 6.5. Knowing a word from hearing parts of it. (Examples: airpla/, tele/one.)
5. *Sound blending.* Jay said "eat" after hearing "m-e."

B. Visual Areas

1. *Visual reception,* age 5.0. (Example: When asked to choose a picture similar to one of a child writing on the board, Jay chose one of a child looking into a mirror instead of the one of a child writing in a notebook.)
2. *Visual memory,* age 6.10. The examiner uses blocks with abstract designs on them. He lays them down in a specified pattern. The child examines for five seconds; then the blocks are mixed up and the child is asked to duplicate the pattern. Jay could do a series of only three.

Frostig Developmental Test of Visual Perception

1. *Visual-motor,* age 7.3. Tests eye-hand coordination. Children often have difficulty in gross motor activities such as ball skills and hopping, or in small motor activities such as writing and cutting. They often appear awkward and clumsy, perhaps have difficulty copying from the board.
2. *Perceptual constancy,* age 6.3. The ability to perceive an object as having certain properties, such as shape and size, in spite of the size of the image on the retina. The child who lacks this perception may not realize that the car down the street is the same size as the one that he is standing next to. He may think that the cars he sees from above are in reality toy cars. He may not perceive that the cup on the table, the one upside down on the counter, and the one hanging in the cupboard are the same objects. His world can be pretty confusing.
3. *Position in space.* The ability to understand the relationship between the observer and the object. The child who lacks this perception may appear clumsy and hesitant in his movements. He is often not sure of where to start in order to move around a desk. He often touches the walls as he walks and bumps into other children. Letters, words, sentences, and number sequences appear distorted and confused. He may reverse *b* and *d, p* and *q, on* and *no, 24* and *42.* Such difficulties also show themselves in the child's lack of awareness of the parts of his own body, their position and function.

Kephart's Perceptual Rating Scale

Jay is left-eyed, right-handed, and right-footed.

1. *Kraus-Weber* tests of physical fitness which have been shown to be directly related to school achievement.
    a. Jay could not raise his head and chest from a prone position with his feet held down.
    b. He could not raise his legs from a prone position. Jay also could not bend over and touch the floor while keeping his knees straight, but this has not been shown to be directly related to school achievement.
2. *Jumping.* Jay could not skip on the right foot, could not hop regular or irregular patterns on alternating feet. This tests laterality, body image, neuromuscular control, rhythm, and body control.
3. *Identification of parts of his body.* Jay did not know where his hips or his ankles were. This was also shown on Frostig *Position in Space*. This shows problems in laterality, directionality, control, rhythm, and spatial localization.
4. *Angels in the Snow.* Abortive movements when moving opposite sides of the body. This showed a specific problem in right- and left-sidedness.
5. *Stepping Stones.* Jay could not adjust to walking the irregularly spaced and distanced foot patterns; this showed a problem in body image, laterality and directionality, and in crossing the midline.
6. *Double circles* were flattened on the inside; this indicated a midline problem.
7. *Vertical lines.* The left one toed in, indicating a laterality problem.
8. *Ocular coordination and pursuit.* Jay could not follow smoothly a moving target in any of the patterns, either monocularly or binocularly.

Valett's *Psychoeducational Inventory of Basic Learning Abilities*

A. Gross Motor
   1. *Weak in balance* in walking a line backward heel to toe.
   2. *Throwing* and catching (Frostig visual-motor indicated same).
   3. *Jumping* rope.
   4. *Skipping*—could not skip on right foot.
   5. *Rhythm,* either free-form or to rock 'n' roll.
   6. *Muscular* strength—could not do a push-up.

B. Sensory-motor
   1. *Laterality* (left eye, right hand and foot).
   2. *Directionality*—did not know left from right, or north-south, east-west.
   3. *Time orientation*—weak in telling time, even by the hour.

C. Perceptual-motor
   1. *Auditory vocal association*—categories and analogies. Could not tell which did not belong in John, Mary, Bill, George."

2. *Visual coordination* and pursuit—eyes did not move together.
3. *Visual figure-ground.* Could not tell whether the wagon was behind the tree (it was by the side). Could not find the four hidden pictures in the water, tree, and flowers.
4. *Visual-motor memory*—inaccurate reproduction of abstract designs after a five-second exposure.
5. *Visual-motor fine-muscle coordination.* Manuscript writing letters incorrectly formed, size inconsistent.

D. Language Development
  1. *Fluency and encoding.* In trying to repeat "Georgie, Porgie, pudding 'n' pie," said, "Georgie, Porgie kissed the made them cry." Could not tell what he wanted for Christmas or his birthday. (Christmas was a month away.)
  2. *Articulation.* Said "brudder" for brother, "yewow" for yellow, "anysing" for anything, "wins" for twins, "rum" for drum. Mispronounced *l, v, r, sh, th, sl, ch.* Said *m* for *n*, and *n* for *m*.
  3. Had no word-attack or spelling skills.

E. Conceptual
  1. *Number concepts, processes, and reasoning.* Jay could count by rote, but only if he started at *1*. He could do simple adding and subtracting on *paper,* but then could not read his answer—that is, say *6, 8, 9,* etc., or any number past *3*. Also, then, he could not write any number dictated out of sequence. He could not make a one-to-one correspondence (he would count faster than he touched or moved objects, and seemed to see no relationship between the words and the action). By the time he had counted to *7,* he had moved or touched only five objects. He *could* tell which group had *more* or *less,* but only through counting them. Written numerals were reversed (*7, 6, 3*), the *4* was written upside down, and the *9* was written as a *g*. He may be stimulus-bound, so that his down stroke is attracted to the circle already made. Jay's reasoning was good orally in that he could tell that if one pencil cost 4¢, then two pencils would cost 8¢, and if Bill got 60¢ allowance a week, he would have more than 60¢ at the end of three weeks if he saved his money. Jay said $1.00.
  2. *General information.* Jay could not tell the name of the nearest grocery store or how to get there. He could not tell the way to get to a friend's house (gestured).
  3. *Classification.* Jay pointed to the picture of the loaf of *bread* as being smaller in real life than either the *flower* or the *bird.* He placed the pictures of the *man, bird,* and *dog* in the same category because they could all breathe. (Should have been the boat, rowboat, motorbike, wagon, car, and plane.)

4. *Comprehension.* Jay could not tell what happens to rivers in the spring of the year, but as he tested high on the WISC comprehension (scaled score 14), one would discount this answer as being a result of his meager environmental stimulation.

F. Social Skills

Social acceptance. Jay is immature at making friends. Very quiet and shy. Is mostly ignored by his peers.

Durrell's *Analysis of Reading Difficulty*

1. Jay could not give the sounds of any single letters, blends, or digraphs.
2. Knew "you-look-tree-come" on the word analysis.

    P   P   P
3. Muff is a little yellow kitten.

  P   P P
She drinks milk.

       P
She sits in/on a chair.

    P   PP   P P
She does not like to get wet.

4. When the examiner sounded out "g-e-t," Jay said "tag."
5. He could mark the correct word when asked to find the one that began like *fall,* or that ended like *crab,* or that had two beginning consonants as *black,* or had beginning and ending consonants as *watch.*

SUMMARY

Jay has no hearing or sight impairment. He has been tested several times by the school nurse. He is stronger in visual than in auditory areas, although there are many problems in the visual areas, too. We would have to classify Jay as a double dyslexic.

Gross Motor. Problems in balance, skipping, jumping, rhythm, muscular strength, and physical fitness, as shown by Kephart and Valett.

Sensory-motor. Problems in laterality, directionality, balance, midline, time orientation, as shown by Kephart and Valett. Coordination same, also shown on *WISC* object assembly.

Perceptual-motor. Problems in associative thinking as shown on *WISC* information (scaled score 7) and similarities (scaled score 7), and *ITPA* auditory reception and association, visual reception, and visual-motor association. Problems in visual coordination and pursuit shown on the Kephart and Valett. Problems in visual-motor memory shown on the Frostig, Valett, and Kephart.

Language Development. Problems in articulation, repeating a series of concepts, sequencing a story, or telling an experience (Durrell and Valett). Weak in classifying and categorizing (*ITPA* and Valett) and in *WISC* object assembly.

REMEDIATION

From December 1969 to June 1970, Jay worked for a half-hour daily after his second grade class had been dismissed, because there was no time slot to work with him. From September 1970 to March 1971, he worked in the Learning Disability Group room two periods daily for a total of ninety minutes with three other children. Work was planned to take advantage of his strengths and to strengthen his weaknesses.

Gross Motor

1. Hopping regular and irregular patterns to a metronome, clapping, or music.
2. Step-hopping (beginning of a skip) to a metronome, clapping, or music, with hands held in front, in back, on head, with right hand up, left hand down, out to the sides, etc. This was done partly to ease the tension of learning to hop and to work on directionality at the same time, to increase his concepts of *before, after, to the side of, behind,* etc.
3. Jumping rope—to increase his self-image, motor coordination, and directionality.
4. Turning somersaults to learn how to control his body and to increase his awareness of position in space.
5. Doing push-ups for physical fitness.
6. Throwing and catching with a Nerf ball against the wall and at a target.
7. Throwing with various balls (stocking, texture, five-inch and ten-inch rubber). Catching.
8. Ring-toss for coordination.
9. Dancing to rock 'n' roll music (balance and directionality).
10. Enrollment in Motor Coordination Class, October, 1970. Jay has missed attending these since Christmas because family is too tired on Monday nights, and because of illnesses, including asthma, flu, and chickenpox.
11. Card list of exercises to work on at home, accompanied by a tag calendar on which he could record the exercises that he worked on.

Sensory-motor

1. Work on balance through use of boards with a curved bottom.
2. Directionality through balancing boards, walking stilts where he said "left-right" as he used each foot; walking a line heel-toe backward; walking on irregularly placed footprints as he said "left-right"; matching left- and right-hand patterns as he said "left-right."
3. Suspendable-ball activities saying "left-right" or using that side of his body as called for by the instructor (right foot, left hand, right shoulder, etc.)
4. Imitating movements of teacher and others ("statue").
5. Following directions as, "Stand in front of the chair; take two steps to the left, three steps to the right," etc.
6. Learning to tell time through the reading of the "invisible minutes."

Perceptual-motor

A. Visual Coordination and Pursuit
   1. Following moving targets—such as a penlight, toy car, thumbtack in the end of a pencil—in horizontal, vertical, diagonal, and rotary patterns.
   2. Peripheral vision—while he was looking straight ahead, see how soon he could name a toy being moved closer to him either from the right or from the left.

B. Auditory Training
   1. Sound blending—blending sounds into a word after hearing them said separately by the teacher or on tape.
   2. Marking the correct word from several after hearing the separate sounds on tape.
   3. Simultaneously listening to, saying, and tracing kinesthetic letters and numbers (using a tape recorder or a record player).
   4. Simultaneously listening to a recording, saying, and walking on the letters or numbers on the floor (or hopping, jumping).
   5. Repeating Morselike code patterns after hearing them.
   6. Repeating sound patterns after hearing them on the buzzer board.

C. Other Visual Training
   1. Frostig exercises, areas I, III, IV, preceded by motor exercises.
   2. Tachistoscopic materials—marking the correct response from multiple-choice answers after exposure to the symbols (series of numbers, letters, flashed designs).
   3. Constructing Try Task Shapes and blocks into patterns after exposure.
   4. Tangrams.
   5. Parquetry.
   6. Plain inch cubes.
   7. Colored inch cubes.
   8. Pegboard designs.
   9. Continental Press visual-motor materials.

Language Development

A. Valett's *Remediation of Learning Difficulties*
   1. Name everything in the room as fast as you can. All the foods, all the toys.
   2. An airplane goes up and rain falls _____.
   3. Firemen work to put out _____.

B. Continental Press's *Reading and Thinking Skills*
   1. Level 1, classifying by pictures.
   2. Levels 2 and 3 can be read aloud by a nonreader or slow reader in order to gain concepts of organization, categorizing, and classifying.

C. Poetry Experiences
   1. *Let's Say Poetry Together.* Educational Record Sales.
   2. *Play It by Ear,* by Lowell and Stower. Good source for poems.
D. Sequence Cards
   1. *Let's Look at Children.* Educational Testing Service, Princeton, N.J.
   2. Homemade sequence cards made from comic strips and old workbooks.
E. Mirror

   To be used while speaking, for observing articulatory errors.

Reading

1. Catherine Stern's *Structural Reading Series.*
2. Sullivan's reading materials.
3. Stratemeyer's *Linguistic Readers.*
4. Old state texts (Allyn and Bacon) cut apart into individual stories.
5. Send to first grade class for reading. Jay is small, feels it a privilege to go to separate class for reading, does not feel "tainted" or degraded. As he becomes more proficient, he may be able to "tutor" a child next year; doing this will strengthen his own reading skills.
6. Jay had 2½ years under competent teachers and still did not learn to read, so a combination of sight and phonetic reading was prescribed. If his total reading is limited to sight words, even in high school he would not be able to read above a Grade 4–5 level and his spelling would be limited to only those words he could revisualize. The rest would be a hodgepodge of misspellings in which the original words could seldom be identified even by himself at a later time (sometimes after as short a time as five minutes).

Mathematics

1. Number line—walking on it as he hears numbers from a tape or teacher. Use it to add and subtract. "Contact" paper makes an excellent number line on the floor.
2. Kinesthetic numbers to trace as he listens to a record.
3. Manipulative materials such as beans and beansticks, Adsum blocks, Cuisenaire rods, Attribute Games and Problems, boxes of pennies, nickels, and dimes.
4. Adding his own daily score of checkmarks by making a one-to-one correspondence using beans or other materials.
5. Estimating and checking—how many steps to the door, how far he can count while doing an exercise, how many times he could lay a ruler or yardstick down between certain objects, etc.
6. Ten and Out Game—use homemade cards or playing cards.
7. *Uncle Wiggly* and other games where he is to give a number answer and then throw a die and move the number of steps shown on the die.

8. Bingo cards—individual cards give the answer; the combinations are on the bingo cards.
9. Judy Clock—teach time using the invisible minutes.

JAY'S PROGRESS TO DATE

Wide Range Achievement Test

	Reading	*Spelling*	*Arithmetic*
11-13-69	K.3	1.2	1.2
5-7-70	1.4	1.0	2.2
4-12-71	2.5	1.7	3.2

Durrell's *Analysis of Reading Difficulty*

5-7-70: Jay still could not read paragraph 1 orally or silent paragraph 2. He could give the sounds of most of the single letters, but only if he referred to a chart with picture clues.

4-12-71: Read paragraph 1 with four words pronounced for him *(drinks, sleeps, does, wet)*. 100 percent comprehension. Read silent paragraph 2 at low first grade speed and with 92 percent comprehension. Word analysis was low 2. Listening comprehension was at paragraph 3.

Progress Summary:

1. Now skips and hops; can jump rope forward six times without stopping; backward, seven jumps without stopping.
2. Can somersault and do a *fair* push-up, but chest is raised slightly before the hips are raised.
3. Still cannot bend over and touch the floor without bending his knees (lacks four inches).
4. Still poor balance on the balance board.
5. Still some confusion with his left and right hands and feet, but the only reading reversals are *saw* and *was, on* and *no*.

CHAPTER 11
Using the psychoeducational inventory and the developmental task analysis: Mitch

Mitch is an 11½-year-old boy in a special education class for educable mentally retarded children. The diagnostic-prescriptive teacher who conducted this evaluation, the author of this chapter, was Harmenia Kourtjian. This report primarily illustrates how the *Psychoeducational Inventory of Basic Learning Abilities* and the *Developmental Task Analysis* may be used with traditional case study information to provide a number of specific teaching objectives.

IDENTIFICATION DATA

Name: Mitch *Birth date:* October 29, 1959
School: L. *Age:* 11
Program: Elementary Educable Mentally Retarded
Teacher: H. Kourtjian
Place: Classroom
Date: March 23, 24, 25, 1971
Time of evaluation: March 23, 12:00 to 12:30; March 24, 12:00 to 12:30; March 25, 9:00 to 9:45.

PERTINENT HISTORY

Health, Educational, and Psychological Problems

May 25, 1968. The guidance report shows the following test results:

Stanford-Binet Intelligence—chronological age 8.6, mental age 5.10, intelligence quotient 66.
Goodenough Drawing—chronological age 8.6, mental age 5.9, intelligence quotient 68.
Wide Range Achievement—reading K1, Spelling PK7, arithmetic K3.

The following quoted from the interpretation and recommendation in the same report: "Mitch was very inquisitive about things in the room and quite talkative. He tired easily and became restless and easily distracted. He has immature speech. He had difficulty in all motor tasks. He achieved a basal age of five years and had success in areas of general comprehension and judgment and reasoning in year seven."

November 29, 1965. The report of the N. School District provides the following information:

Test used: *Stanford-Binet.*
Test summary: Chronological age 6.1, mental age 4.0, intelligence quotient 62, percentile rank 1%.

Information from school: Mitch lives with his mother and an older brother. In the children's group he is an isolate. In his relations with adults he is defiant. His attendance has been irregular. His health is said to be fair. He has a speech impediment. He seems excessively withdrawn. The teacher says that he may be an underachiever and is emotionally disturbed. She comments: "Mitch is extremely hostile toward his peers, teachers, and the classroom environment. His small-muscle skills are lower than the level of most children in this age group. He is nervous and unhappy in the classroom. He cries constantly and has to be brought into the room forcibly."

Behavior during test: "The over-all testing conditions were only fairly satisfactory. Mitch was exceedingly easily distracted. He was very concerned about going to lunch and about the bells whenever they would ring. He needed a great deal of urging in order to respond. He seemed to be a shy, rather anxious boy. However, he was very much at ease with the examiner and looked to her for reassurance many times during the testing. He tended to give up rather easily."

Evaluation:

Test	*Record*
III-6	42 months
IV	3 months
IV-6	0 months
V	1 month
VI	2 months
VII	0 months
Total	48 months

"Basal age three years six months with scatter through year six. All tests failed at the seven-year level. All tests were also failed at the four-year six-months level, but because the range was so limited he was given the items at years five, six, and seven. At the four-year level he failed *Opposite analogies 1, Pictorial identification,* and *Discrimination of forms* tests. On the *Opposite analogies 1* test, he had one correct response where two are required. On the *Pictorial identification* test he had two correct responses where three are needed. On the *Discrimination of forms* test he had seven correct responses, but eight are required. At year 4.6, where all tests were failed, he had two correct responses on the *Aesthetic comparison* test which requires three for credit. He had two correct responses on the *Pictorial similarities and differences 1* test, but three are needed for credit. At the five-year level, he passed the *Definition* test. He did have one point on the *Picture completion: man* test, but two are needed for credit at this level. At year six he was able to pass the maze test. At the seven-year level, where all tests were failed, he had one correct response on the *Comprehension IV* test, which requires three for credit.

Summary and suggestions: "Mitch's vocabulary was extremely poor and his speech is immature, at times almost unintelligible. He had very poor visual-motor coordination. It would be helpful to know what his relations are with his older brother. It would be important to talk with the mother about his attitudes toward school and his own school achievement. He should learn to have more confidence in his own performance."

May 4, 1966. The teacher's follow-up report on Mitch at age 6.6 is quoted: "Mitch has many friends and a good attitude. He cannot do any work in the classroom but fits in well at recess and P.E. During school time (two hours), he sits and looks around or plays with clay or a toy. Sometimes he strings beads, but would rather sit and watch. He does not object to coming to school now and seems happy."

May 10, 1967. Another follow-up shows that Mitch has little interest in even the simplest activities and that he has a very short attention span. His coordination is not too good, but he enjoys playing games. He likes to be included in a reading group and is most happy when he feels he has succeeded in some work. His speech has shown some improvement. He is easily worried and frightened by loud noises (sonic booms) and stray dogs.

June 12, 1970. Mitch's progress report indicates that he is polite, cooperative, honest, oversensitive, neat, and cries easily when disciplined. "He works well in group situations, is accepted by peers, shares with others, and participates in group activities. He constantly needs praise and reinforcement. He works best on a one-to-one basis and needs a structured classroom situation. He is preoccupied with death, loud noises and fighting . . . he would not use the restroom because he said the monsters were there . . . later found out he was afraid of the toilet noise. He will not stay in the room when blinds and windows are closed and a film is being shown. Claims he has a stomach ache."

May 17, 1966. A medical report shows that Mitch developed jaundice shortly after birth, which was attributed to the mother's being Rh negative; but he made a good recovery and did not require any blood transfusions. From his early development he sat up at the age of eight months, walked when he was fourteen months, and started talking when he was two years old. He seems to have temper tantrums, during which he throws himself down; and he seems very overactive and restless. Mitch's father committed suicide while in prison when Mitch was seven years old. Allegedly, the father had blackout spells, and also on his side of the family there were epilepsy and asthma. Mitch seems to have few friends, and he may play by himself happily all the time. He seems to be restless and overactive most of the time, and at times he presents an explosive type of activity. He seems unable to sit down and has frequent temper tantrums. He has a tendency to wet his bed when he has any illnesses like colds, flu, etc. In school his coordination is poor; and he seems to be weaker on the left side, and especially on the left leg. In school he does very poorly. He cannot read and write and is far behind the other children in class. He attends school only half-time because he claims he gets very tired. His coordination is so poor that even at times when he walks, he falls down very easily. The neurological examination revealed that Mitch was tense and restless. At times he assumes a rigid position and other times he has an explosive activity. It is difficult to get him to cooperate, and he actually gives no information about himself but relies entirely on his mother. The left leg seemed to be weaker than the right, and the deep tendon reflexes appeared to be mildly asymmetric and weaker on the left leg. Diagnostically, the physician felt "this child has a case of severe cerebral dysrhythmia and also, because of his weakness of the left leg, I feel that he has a mild case of cerebral palsy."

Reason for Referral and Evaluation

Mitch is a delightful child and tries hard to succeed. His areas of weakness are primarily in the academic subjects of reading, writing, and arithmetic. There are days when he is even unable to write his name and do routine classroom activities. I felt that a case study for this child would be beneficial so that I would know more of how I could help him in the classroom.

EVALUATION PROCEDURE

The instruments employed are: (1) *A Psychoeducational Inventory of Basic Learning Abilities* and (2) *Developmental Task Analysis*. The *Inventory* is a task analysis sampling covering a range of developmental areas. It samples step-by-step the six major areas of learning: (1) gross motor development; (2) sensory-motor integration; (3) perceptual-motor skills of auditory perception, visual perception, and visual-motor perception; (4) language development; (5) conceptual skills; and (6) social skills. The purpose of the *Developmental Task Analysis* is to obtain by means of parental judgment and response the level of accomplishment of various behavioral tasks in the following areas: (1) social and personal skills, (2) motor skills, (3) perceptual skills, (4) language skills, and (5) thinking skills.

Pupil Attitude, Motivation, and General Behavior

Mitch displayed excessive motor activity and short attention span during the evaluation. After doing item 6M in the Gross Motor Development section, he continually wanted to throw paper balls into the wastebasket. Also, he was not too happy during the evaluation and kept asking, "When can I go out to play? I want to play."

Testing Environment

The evaluation of the *Developmental Task Analysis* was in the home by the parent. I did the evaluation of the *Inventory* in the classroom while the other children were out. The room was quiet and, except for one student who returned to the room to get his jacket, there were no distractions.

Appropriateness and Validity of Instruments

The *Developmental Task Analysis* was appropriate in that it provided, by means of parental judgment, a profile of tasks that are learned well, partially learned, beginning to be learned, and those not yet begun to be learned. I do not feel that it was completely valid, however, in that it was inconsistent in the evaluating.

The *Inventory* was also appropriate, as it provided a profile of learning disabilities and strengths through sample tasks in the fifty-three basic learning abilities, which is helpful in diagnosing and planning an educational program with priority learning tasks. Again, I feel it was not completely valid, due to the pupil's lack of motivation and concentration.

SUMMARY OF SCORES

Developmental Task Analysis

	0	1	2	3	Total
Social and Personal Skills	3	0	5	15	23
Motor Skills	2	0	3	12	17
Perceptual Skills	4	1	7	7	19
Language Skills	8	0	3	4	15
Thinking Skills	5	0	4	11	20
TOTALS	22	1	22	49	94

Psychoeducational Inventory of Basic Learning Abilities

	Very Weak	Weak	Average	Strong	Very Strong	Total
Gross Motor Development	2	2.5	5	1.5	3	14
Sensory-motor Integration	0	4.5	1.5	1	0	7
Perceptual-motor Skills	2.5	7.5	2	1	2	15
Language Development	4	1.5	1.5	0	0	7
Conceptual Skills	1.5	2	2.5	0	0	6
Social Skills	0	1	.5	1.5	1	4
						53

PERFORMANCE INTERPRETATION

The *Developmental Task Analysis* shows that in the area of social and personal skills, Mitch has not yet begun to learn self-control; participation in clubs, teams, or social groups; and to assume personal and social responsibility in family, school, and neighborhood. He has partially learned with some difficulties how to care for himself without demanding unusual attention; he attends to and completes various tasks (playing baseball and catch with older brother, fourteen). He has partially learned to help other people, to show empathy toward them, to be courteous and pleasant toward others, and to accept constructive criticism. The following items are well learned with no difficulties: is aware of self and of effect on others; is aware of and responds to parents when present; acknowledges friends and siblings; plays constructively by self with toys; smiles and laughs when stimulated by others; plays with other children and adults; shares and cooperates in play; plays simple competitive games, such as dominoes, with others; cares for animals or other favorite objects (puppy and his baseball glove); helps with simple family chores and tasks by cleaning his room and throwing out the trash; has special interests or hobbies—he is an avid baseball and football fan and watches all games on television; has several friends and is popular with other children—has a girlfriend and also two cousins that he likes; he is generally honest and straightforward; has a sense of right and wrong that guides his behavior; and attends school full time—when he is not sick.

In the area of *motor skills* (body movement and control), Mitch has not yet begun to learn to tie his shoes and jump rope. He has partially learned with some difficulty to wash and bathe himself, to dress himself, and to cut paper with blunt scissors. The following are tasks that are learned well in this area: crawling; walking without aid or support; walking up and down stairs; jumping over small obstacles; running around the yard; throwing and catching a rubber ball; skipping back and forth; caring for self at toilet; completes coloring book pictures with crayons; rides bicycle; participates in informal neighborhood and school sports such as baseball, kickball, and dodgeball; and can move about the neighborhood or community without supervision.

In the area of *perceptual skills* (listening-seeing-doing), Mitch has not yet begun to learn how to repeat a poem or simple song, to write the ABC's, or to thread a needle through a buttonhole; and he does have a noticeable visual handicap. He still makes reversals and/or writes backward; however, this task is beginning to be learned with many difficulties and little accomplishment. He has partially learned with some difficulties to match letters, numbers, and simple words; to say the ABC's by name when presented out of order; to draw recognizable figures and pictures with pencil; to print his name; to write numbers 1–30; to sort out different buttons quickly; and to write his name with good handwriting.

In the area of *language skills* (vocabulary understanding and speech), Mitch has not begun to learn and rejects the task of explaining simple arithmetic problems, speaking with no articulation or other speech difficulties, reading simple words, spelling simple words, writing his address and city; writing simple letters and sentences, using the telephone book and making calls, and completing business applications. He has partially learned with some difficulties to imitate sounds and words and to describe events or objects with fluency, and he has a limited vocabulary. The following are items that are learned well with no difficulties: pointing to simple objects in pictures as requested; talking in sentences; defining simple words such as "hot," "apples," and "letter"; and reading appropriate school books. (I am aware of the inconsistency in the evaluation; however, for our purposes, I am simply proceeding on the parent's evaluation.)

In the area of *thinking skills*, the pupil does not know the months of the year, the four seasons, telling time to the quarter hour, how to do multiplication, and how to purchase things at the store. He has partially learned with some difficulty the parts of the human body, to do simple addition and subtraction, and to explain the rules of baseball and football. The following tasks are learned well with no difficulties: knows basic colors; remembers what happened yesterday; can count pennies to twenty; knows nickel, dime, and quarter; can sort big and little sticks; knows the top and bottom of a box; understands "in" and "out"; knows left and right; understands loud and soft; understands jokes and/or riddles; and understands "city," "state," and "nation."

The profile of the *Psychoeducational Inventory* indicates that Mitch has few strengths and many disabilities. In the area of *gross motor development,* Mitch shows disabilities in throwing accurately, skipping alternately, and body abstractions. He is weak to average in controlled rolling, jumping obstacles, and dancing. He is average in coordinated walking, muscular strength (sit-ups, leg-ups, bends), and general physical health. He is average to strong in body localization (part location). He shows strengths in sitting erect, crawling smoothly, running a course, and self-identification (name awareness).

In *sensory-motor integration,* Mitch shows weakness in balance and rhythm, directionality, laterality (hand, eye, foot), and time orientation (lapse and concept). He is weak to average in reaction-speed dexterity and average in tactile discrimination (object identification), and shows strengths in body-spatial organization.

In *perceptual-motor skills* Mitch shows weakness in auditory-vocal association, auditory sequencing (imitative response), visual acuity (Snellen), visual coordination and pursuit, visual figure-ground differentiation, visual-motor memory (designs), fine muscle coordination, visual-motor spatial-form manipulation (blocks), visual-motor speed of learning (coding), and visual-motor integration (draw-a-man). He is average in auditory acuity (functional hearing). He is average to strong in visual-form discrimination (association) and in visual memory (visual recall). He shows strengths in auditory decoding (following directions) and in auditory memory (retention).

In *language development,* the pupil shows weakness in vocabulary, word-attack skills (phonic association), reading comprehension, writing, and spelling. He is weak to average in articulation, and average in fluency and encoding. He does not show any strengths in this area.

In *conceptual skills,* Mitch is weak in the arithmetic processes of addition, subtraction, multiplication, and division; in arithmetic reasoning (problem solving); and in classification (relationships). He is weak to average in number concepts (counting). He is average in general information and in comprehension (common-sense reasoning). He does not show any strengths in this area.

In *social skills,* Mitch shows weakness in social acceptance. He is average to strong in value judgments (ethical-moral sense), and he shows strengths in anticipatory response (foresight) and in social maturity (gross problem solving).

SPECIFIC STRENGTHS

The *Developmental Task Analysis* indicates that Mitch has abilities in most *social* and *personal skills,* with the exception of self-control, group and club participation, and assuming personal and social responsibility in family, school, and neighborhood. He is beginning to learn to get along without unusual care and attention, attending to and completing various tasks, helping other people, being courteous and pleasant toward others, and accepting constructive criticism.

He also shows abilities in most *motor skills,* with the exception of tying shoes and jumping rope. He is beginning to learn to wash and bathe himself, to dress himself, and to cut paper with blunt scissors.

The profile also indicates that Mitch has abilities in *thinking skills,* with the exception of knowing the months of the year, the four seasons, telling time, doing multiplication, and purchasing things at the store. He is beginning to learn to explain the rules of baseball and football, to do simple addition and subtraction, and to identify body parts.

In the area of *perceptual skills,* Mitch has specific abilities in responding to sound and musical toys; replying appropriately to simple directions; repeating simple words, numbers, and sentences; focusing eyes on picture or storybook; using silverware at the table; building block houses; and using hammer and nails and other tools. He has partially learned with some difficulty to match letters, numbers, and simple words; the letters of the alphabet when presented out of order; to draw recognizable figures and pictures with pencil; to print his name; to write numbers 1–30; to sort buttons; and to write his name with good handwriting.

The profiles of the *Psychoeducational Inventory* indicate that Mitch has abilities in sitting erectly, crawling smoothly, running a course, self-identification, body localization, body-spatial organization, decoding (following directions), memory retention, form discrimination, memory (visual recall), anticipatory response, value judgments, and social maturity.

SPECIFIC WEAKNESSES

The profiles of the *Developmental Task Analysis* indicate that Mitch has learning disabilities in all areas of *language skills,* with the exception of reading appropriate schoolbooks; defining words such as "hat," "apple," and "letter";

talking in sentences; and pointing to simple objects. These items have been learned well with no difficulties. He has partially learned with some difficulty how to imitate sounds and words, to establish a limited vocabulary, and to describe events or objects with fluency. Areas of weakness in *perceptual skills* include the inability to repeat a poem or simple song, to write the ABC's, or to thread a needle through buttonholes, and a visual handicap. There is a doubt regarding Mitch's ability to match duplicate pictures or playing cards, to assemble simple jigsaw puzzles, and to tie knots in a rope.

The profiles of the *Psychoeducational Inventory* indicate that Mitch has learning disabilities in controlled rolling, throwing accurately, jumping, skipping alternately, dancing, body abstraction, balance and rhythm, reaction-speed dexterity, directionality, laterality, time orientation, vocal association, sequencing, visual acuity, coordination and pursuit, figure-ground differentiation, visual-motor memory, fine muscle coordination, spatial-form manipulation, speed of learning (coding), and integration (draw-a-man). In *language development* he shows disabilities in all areas, with the exception of fluency and encoding and articulation. On these items his performance is average. In *conceptual skills* Mitch has weaknesses in all areas, with the exception of general information and comprehension. His performance on these items is average. On *number concepts* his performance is weak to average. The only area of weakness in *social skills* is in social acceptance (friendship).

IMPLICATIONS AND RECOMMENDATIONS

Priority Learning Tasks

On the basis of the combined evaluation, priority learning tasks should include the following:

1. Teach names of the letters of the alphabet.
2. Teach Dolch's Basic Sight Words.
3. Provide practice in developing writing ability.
4. Teach number concepts of more and less.
5. Have the pupil participate in speech demonstration stories. (Already receives speech therapy.)

Prescriptive-programming Suggestions

1. Use the kinesthetic alphabet to teach the names of the letters.
2. Devote five minutes a day teaching the basic sight words.
3. Present pupil with review of right-to-left exercises using scribbles, arrows, and straight-line drawings.
4. Have pupil trace his name in wet sand.
5. Use thin rolls of clay to make letters and to write his name.
6. Have Mitch trace his name, using onionskin; also, numbers, letters, and designs. Follow by having him trace again with crayon and then pencil.

7. On chalkboard, introduce letters L/I/T/H/O, indicating directions of strokes. Have Mitch copy with a felt pen and crayons. Gradually introduce entire alphabet and numbers. Use extensive practice and success before proceeding to the next letter.
8. Give Mitch a piece of candy, have him eat it, and ask if he wants more. Then give him two more pieces. Arrange one piece of candy and three pieces of candy and ask which is more? Which is less? Group three and six pieces and repeat questions.
9. Show pictures of drawings of familiar objects. Have the pupil circle picture with more objects and fewer objects.
10. Use pictures and seasons for speech sounds, such as Christmas, Easter, etc.

Other Comments and Impressions

The visit with the parent was especially valuable, because she could personalize and tell things not necessarily included on a task analysis. As a result of this experience, I feel that I understand Mitch just a little bit better.

CHAPTER 12

Applying diagnostic findings to prescriptive suggestions: Robbie

Robbie is a boy age nine years and four months in a program for educationally handicapped children. The diagnostic-prescriptive evaluation was done by Diana Robinson, a graduate student in learning disabilities who was serving as Robbie's tutor through a graduate practicum assignment; she is the author of this chapter. The case illustrates another approach in the use and interpretation of inventories and task-analysis instruments. It also shows how diagnostic findings can be related to specific prescriptive suggestions from *The Remediation of Learning Disabilities.**

FINDINGS

    I. Gross Motor Development[1]

    Strengths:
        1. Rolling—except the somersault.
        2. Sitting.
        5. Running.
        6. Throwing.
      10. Self-identification.
      11. Body localization—except for the advanced task, "What are eyes (hands, stomach) for?" Robbie did not give a very verbal answer.

    Average:
        3. Crawling—had trouble with cross-lateral and with spoon and bead.
        4. Walking—wobbly backwards.
      12. Body abstraction—"When you grow up what do you think you will look like?" "Don't know." When I asked, "What will change?" he said, "your face."
      13. Muscular strength—did not exert himself, and was panting.

---

*Valett, Robert, *The Remediation of Learning Disabilities, A Handbook of Psychoeducational Resource Programs,* Fearon Publishers/Lear Siegler, Inc., Education Division, 6 Davis Drive, Belmont, California 94002.

1. The organization of this material, in particular the enumeration of items, is based on *A Psychoeducational Inventory of Basic Learning Abilities.* See Chapter 7.

Weak in:

7. Jumping—rope forward and backward.
8. Skipping—forward and backward with the rope.
9. Dancing—when marching, got off beat. (I did not have a record player to do the other two tasks.)
14. General physical health—told me what to do if you cut your finger: "Put a band-aid on it." But said "Don't know" for the type of food that should be in a balanced diet, and for why it is important to get lots of sleep and exercise.

These findings correlate with Robbie's scores on the *Inventory of Primary Skills*[2] in self-information, body identification, and draw-a-man, on which he did well for his age.

In the Developmental Task Analysis:[3]

1. His parents marked 3's on all tasks *except* "participates in informal neighborhood or school sports" and "participates in formal competitive athletics." They noted that he has only one or two friends and would rather come home and work on his rabbit hutch than stay at school.
2. Robbie's teacher was not sure of many of the tasks, but noted that he cannot clap in a steady rhythm, which I, too, noted in his marching.

II. Sensory-motor integration

Strong in:

15. Balance and rhythm—a little wobbly.
16. Body-spatial organization.
18. Tactile discrimination.
19. Directionality—mixed up east and west.
20. Laterality.

Average:

17. Reaction-speed dexterity—took a long time.

Weak in:

21. Time orientation—off beat for jumping up and down as I clapped; said "summer" for Easter and Halloween, then changed them to "spring" and "winter."

On the *Inventory of Primary Skills,* Robbie also did well with body-spatial relations. But he did very poorly with directionality on both body identification and position-in-space concepts.

2. *An Inventory of Primary Skills,* Chapter 6.
3. *Developmental Task Analysis,* Chapter 5.

These findings correlate with those from the *Developmental Task Analysis* in that his teacher said Robbie could not keep a rhythm clapping and later mentioned that he does not know his seasons.

III. Perceptual-motor skills

Did well on:

22. Auditory acuity.
23. Auditory decoding.
26. Auditory sequencing—except for the task of repeating "School starts in September . . ." He left out about half of the words.
28. Visual coordination and pursuit.
29. Visual-form discrimination.
31. Visual memory.
32. Visual-motor memory.
33. Visual-motor fine muscle coordination.

Average:

24. Auditory-vocal association—way down on verbal expression.
25. Auditory memory—did well until it came to "Tell me your favorite story." He said, "I don't have one."
27. Visual acuity—again not very verbal.
30. Visual figure-ground differentiation—had a hard time finding the hidden objects, and circled "giv" and "ing."
34. Visual-motor spatial-form manipulation—wrote his last name wrong, and erased many times in copying the picture.
36. Visual-motor integration—family all looked the same except that the children were smaller; missed one part of the design, and wrote "met" instead of "meat."

Weak in:

35. Visual-motor speed of learning—Task B, marked about 39; Task M, kept dropping the nuts and bolts—about two minutes; Task A, stopped halfway through and worked from right to left on the last word—about two minutes.

Robbie's visual and auditory acuity were tested at the beginning of November. He was alert in responding to all tones in the speech range at 5-10 decibels. His vision was 20/20 on the Snellen chart.

His good performance on visual-form discrimination and average performance on visual figure-ground differentiation correlate with his good performance on symbol matching and position-in-space concepts on the *Inventory of Primary Skills.*

On the *Developmental Task Analysis* the teacher noted that Robbie often makes reversals in reading—"on" for "no." His parents noted his good handwriting.

The scores on the *Illinois Test of Psycholinguistic Abilities* indicate that Robbie did well on auditory memory (age score 10-3, ss 38, +3.5) and visual memory (10-5, 38, +3.5). But on the *ITPA,* Robbie did poorly on auditory decoding (8-4, 30, -4.5), whereas he did well on the *Psychoeducational Inventory.* Also, on the *Inventory* he performed average on auditory-vocal association, but well on the *ITPA* (10-11, 42, +7.5).

IV. Language Development

Strengths:

37. Vocabulary—missed "kangaroo" and "stethoscope" on Task A.
39. Articulation.

Average:

38. Fluency and encoding—weak in verbal expression and repeating sentence.
40. Word-attack skills—circled "ing" and "mor."
42. Writing—"then" for "the," "kote" for "caught."

Weak in:

41. Reading comprehension—misread Task B, and terrible reading of paragraph, but got one question right.
43. Spelling—"grle" for "girl"; "ram"—arm; "woch"—watch; "srcl"—circle; "pinet"—picnic; "arpan"—airplane; "scie"—sky; "prsn"—person; "hows"—house; "krtmrs"—Christmas.

These findings correlate with a low score on sight vocabulary in the *Inventory of Primary Skills.* However, on this measure he did well on paragraph reading and sentence copying.

Robbie's self-evaluation revealed, again, his low verbal fluency.

His lack of verbal expression showed up also on the *ITPA* (5-8, 24, -10.5).

The *Developmental Task Analysis* also revealed his reading and spelling deficit.

1. His parents marked all tasks 3, except reading appropriate school books. They noted that he had a hard time reading up to grade level. His father said he used to help Robbie with reading by having him sound out the word, but now he would much rather work with Robbie's younger brother because he catches on much quicker.
2. Robbie's teacher marked 3's on about half of the tasks. She marked 3's on fluency, articulation, reading and spelling simple words, reading appropriate school books, writing letters and sentences. She noted that Robbie's main problem is in spelling and reading.

V. Conceptual Skills

Strong in:

44. Number concepts.

Average in:

45. Arithmetic processes—did all right on addition and subtraction but poorly on multiplication and division.
46. Arithmetic reasoning—tried to do it all in his head.
47. General information—had a hard time describing South Viet Nam, and could not tell me what a city council does.

Weaknesses:

48. Classification—circled the pumpkin for the smallest object; underlined the man and dog for the largest. Did not get any of the objects with the same purpose, and could not tell me to what classification the objects belonged.
49. Comprehension—low on verbal expression. On question about what happens to rivers in spring, Robbie answered that they dry up. For explaining baseball, he told me a joke instead: "What has eighteen feet and catches flies?"

The *Developmental Task Analysis* showed:

1. The teacher was concerned about Robbie not being able to remember what happened yesterday, not knowing his months or seasons, telling time, multiplication, and not having a notion of city, state, or nation.
2. The parents were not concerned about anything, but noted his good memory for details (which showed up on perceptual-motor skills also).

On the Inventory of Primary Skills, Robbie did well on counting, writing numbers, and recognizing numbers, and did average to good on arithmetic processes. But on this measure he did well (14 out of 14) on class concepts, which involves classification. However, the *Psychoeducational Inventory* required him to group a number of objects and give the classification name, whereas the *Inventory of Primary Skills* only required him to pick out objects after being given the name of the classification.

VI. Social skills

Average:

50. Social acceptance.
53. Social maturity.

Poor:

51. Anticipatory response.
52. Value judgments.

On the *Developmental Task Analysis,* Robbie's parents marked 2's on "Helps with simple family chores and tasks," "Attends to and completes various tasks," "Demonstrates self-control," "Participates in clubs, teams, or social groups," and

"Accepts constructive criticism." They marked ones on "Has several friends and is popular with others" and "Assumes personal and social responsibility in family, school, and neighborhood." They noted that he does not get along well with his neighbors, and that he has only one or two friends because he is always fighting. They also mentioned his bashfulness. Robbie had run out the back door when I came in, and his mother said that he probably would not be back until I left.

Robbie's teacher marked 2's on "Has some special interests or hobbies," "Has several friends and is popular with others," "Is generally honest and straightforward," "Has a sense of right and wrong that guides his behavior," "Helps other people and shows empathy," and "Assumes personal and social responsibility in family, school, and neighborhood." She mentioned that Robbie will participate in group activities, if he does not think he will fail. But if he thinks he will fail, he tries to hide so he won't have to be chosen; or if already in the group, he stops trying.

ROBBIE'S AREAS OF CONCERN

I. Developmental Task Analysis—Parents

1. Social and personal skills—popularity and responsibilities in school, family, and neighborhood.
2. Motor skills—participation in sports.
3. Language skills—reading.

II. Developmental Task Analysis—Teacher

1. Social and personal skills—popularity, helping others, responsibilities in school, participation in group activities.
2. Motor skills—coordination in clapping in rhythm.
3. Perceptual skills—reversals in reading.
4. Language skills—fluency, reading, spelling, and writing.
5. Conceptual skills—months, seasons, city, state, and nation.

III. Inventory of Primary Skills

1. Directionality—right/left hands and feet.
2. Sight vocabulary—reading and sounding out.
3. Paragraph reading—reading slowly and with many mistakes.

IV. Illinois Test of Psycholinguistic Abilities

1. Verbal expression—vocal encoding and fluency.
2. Auditory closure—ability to fill in missing parts of orally presented words and to produce the complete word.
3. Auditory reception—decoding, ability to derive meaning from orally presented material, ability to comprehend the spoken word.

4. Visual closure—ability to identify a common object from an incomplete visual representation.
5. Grammatic closure—ability to make use of the redundancies of oral language, eliciting the ability to respond automatically to often-repeated expressions.

V. Self-Evaluation

1. Verbal expression—fluency. Robbie described things in as few words as possible and could think of no more.
2. Creativity—divergent thinking.
3. Gave expected response—stopped and thought about his answers before responding; said what he thought you wanted to hear.

VI. Psychoeducational Inventory of Basic Learning Abilities

1. Gross-motor development—jumping, skipping, dancing, general physical health.
2. Sensory-motor integration—time orientation.
3. Perceptual-motor skills—visual-motor speed of learning.
4. Language development—reading comprehension, spelling.
5. Conceptual skills—classification, comprehension.
6. Social skills—anticipatory response, value judgments.

REMEDIATION

Priorities for Remediation

As Robbie's tutor, the areas that I am most concerned about, my priorities for remediation, are:[4]

1. Vocabulary—the ability to understand words.
2. Reading comprehension—the ability to understand what you have read.
3. Spelling—the ability to spell in both oral and written form.
4. Verbal expression—fluency and encoding.
5. Classification—the ability to recognize class identities and to use them in establishing logical relationships.
6. Social skills—value judgments, the ability to recognize and respond to moral and ethical issues; social acceptance, the ability to get along with one's peers.
7. Gross motor skills—jumping, skipping, dancing.
8. Time orientation—the ability to judge lapses in time and to be aware of time concepts, months, and seasons.

---

4. See Robert E. Valett, *The Remediation of Learning Disabilities* (Belmont, Calif.: Fearon Publishers, 1967).

Ideas for Remediation

1. *Vocabulary* develops as a result of experience and neurological integration, so children should be provided with varied educational opportunities. Beginning teaching of vocabulary requires concrete aids, imitation, and reinforcement techniques.[5] Robbie has no trouble repeating or imitating sounds or words; his trouble lies in reading and writing the words, and in the size of his vocabulary. Robbie needs help mainly in his sight vocabulary, so I plan to begin by associating words with pictures, in the hope that he will learn to recognize a word if he sees it in another situation. Using kinesthetic tracing and sand letters to reinforce vocabulary and having Robbie cut out pictures for a picture-manuscript vocabulary file are two additional ideas for remediation of Robbie's low vocabulary.

2. *Comprehension of reading material* requires an accurate vocabulary knowledge and the ability to relate words meaningfully in sentence, paragraph, and story form. Comprehension is developed through feedback and consideration of what has just been read.[6] Since Robbie has such a limited vocabulary, it takes him so long to read a simple paragraph that when he gets to the end he has forgotten the first part. Ideas for helping Robbie are to have him group words by category (classification); have him put little words together to make new words; have him read a sentence, discuss the meaning, then draw a picture depicting the meaning; increase the length of the sentence every day; introduce a typewriter and let him spell and write with it. Suggested materials: Sullivan Series, programmed texts, Password, and Word Bingo. For further evaluation I am in the process of giving Robbie the Spache Diagnostic Reading Test.

3. *Spelling* requires visual-motor integration, basic vocabulary knowledge, and phonic awareness.[7] Robbie uses phonics to help him sound out unfamiliar words, but tries to use phonics, incorrectly, for spelling. Examples of his spelling mistakes: uv—of, helth—health, hete—heat, sum—some, riel—real, lafe—laugh, misk—mix, hlud—held, tei—tea, woch—watch, spid—spend. I think he needs help with his spelling rules. Since he tries to use the phonics method, but incorrectly, I would like to try the whole-word method for a while to see if that helps. I also plan to use the method of writing a word, having him trace it on paper, then "write" it in the air from memory, then copy the word on paper, and finally write the word from memory. I also plan to do the same for simple sentences.

4. Fluent *verbal expression* and communication develop gradually as a result of experience and verbal stimulation.[8] Robbie does not come from a very verbal home background, which I feel has influenced his bashfulness and quiet attitude. He needs to be given the opportunity to express himself, each time being rewarded and encouraged so he will feel freer to express himself at other times. Having him work on associations and describing objects and pictures would be a good

---

5. *Ibid.*, Program 37.
6. *Ibid.*, Program 41.
7. *Ibid.*, Program 43.
8. *Ibid.*, Program 38.

beginning, giving him lots of verbal and visual clues. Then, once his self-esteem is raised, I would have him make up sentences and stories. Play-acting, guessing games, and picture reading are good exercises for increasing verbal fluency.

5. *Classification* concepts develop gradually, beginning with simple likenesses and differences and progressing up to formal logical thought, from sensory-motor and concrete stages to recognizing relationships inherent in groupings and classification systems.[9] To develop this concept, I should start with having Robbie match concrete items, and then would have him group several items together. Each time, the reasons for putting certain items together should be explained to him, or by him. I would gradually work up to identifying and categorizing symbolic elements, varying the types of classifications. For complex categories, I would begin with same-colored forms, then have him make subgroupings of broad categories.

6. To help Robbie develop better *social skills,* I would like to gradually introduce more children into our tutoring sessions, to help him learn to share and to have patience, and to help him in successful competition. Social acceptance is of utmost importance to Robbie at this time. First he needs to develop a better picture of himself, which will probably come with success in school. Robbie does not have very many friends, and his parents mentioned that he often fights, so self-control, cooperation, and good manners should come next.

7. Robbie's *gross motor coordination* in the areas of jumping, skipping, and rhythm need to be worked on. He seemed to enjoy the gross motor part of the evaluation, so I think I will have him do one or two of these tasks as a study break every day. Robbie is often quite visibly nervous, so maybe if he had the opportunity to burn off some of that excess energy he could perform better on academic tasks.

8. To help Robbie with *time orientation,* I plan to utilize his good memory and arithmetic ability. He has trouble with rhythm, and with the months and seasons. To teach the concept of months, I plan to begin with minutes and go on to days, to weeks, to months; and then, to teach seasons by saying that a certain number of months constitute a season, and so on. The use of pictures, holidays, vacations, sports, hunting game, and the like facilitate the learning of months and seasons.

9. *Ibid.,* Program 48.

CHAPTER 13

Behavior records and the specification of objectives: T. W.

T. W. is a sixteen-year-old speech-handicapped pupil who attends regular high-school classes. She has received individual speech and language therapy supplemental to her regular school program for a number of years. The therapist conducting this evaluation and prescriptive program was Susan Gililland, author of this chapter. This case illustrates the use of behavior records such as baseline and intervention charting in speech- and language-development programs. It is also an excellent example of the specification of language learning objectives and how they may be achieved through the use of prescriptive teaching, family involvement, and positive-reinforcement techniques.

BACKGROUND INFORMATION

The subject, a sixteen-year-old girl, is a high-school sophomore who has had several years of speech therapy through the public-school system. She is an arrested hydrocephalic and even though she is able to attend regular classes, has much difficulty "passing" and making friends. She appears to be very self-conscious about her speech problem and, in general, it is felt that a correction of her frontal lisp will enhance her personality and perhaps increase the number of her friends.

The subject (hereafter referred to as T. W.) was tested with the use of several tools to determine a starting point for her remedial training program. The Templin-Darley, McDonald Deep Test of Articulation, a tape-recorded speech sample, and a sound-discrimination test were utilized as diagnostic tools. Also, a quick stimulability test assured the clinician that T. W. was a good candidate for a closely structured learning program.

BASELINE DATA

A baseline was established during the first three hours of speech therapy with the initial evaluation and testing period utilized for this purpose. T. W. was seen twice weekly for a period of thirty minutes each session. In total, she has been seen eight hours over a period of nine weeks beginning with the week of March 8, 1971, up to the present date, May 5, 1971.

The behavior selected for observation was the number of correctly produced sibilant sounds and the number of incorrectly produced sibilant sounds for each thirty-minute session. A running tabulation sheet was kept for each session for the entire eight hours of therapy to check the progress and effectiveness of the treatment program: only the first three hours of therapy are indicated on the baseline chart (Figure 14).

A ten-minute tape-recorded sample of spontaneous speech was used for the baseline along with prepared sentences that were read. The sentences are similar to those used in the McDonald Deep Test of Articulation—Sentence Form. For a list of the sentences used see Appendix I of this chapter.

The baseline indicated an average of 54+ incorrectly produced sibilant sounds in contrast with eight correctly produced sibilant sounds for each thirty-minute session. This ratio is 1.8/.26 per minute, with incorrect sibilants over correct sibilants.

OBJECTIVE

The objective of the proposed program was to teach correct production of the sibilant sounds (/s/ and /z/) so that they can be produced easily and at will in all connected speech.

As a specific target behavior, the subject was to produce correctly articulated sibilant sounds of predetermined words, phrases, and sentences: 45 out of 50 responses were to be correctly emitted in a structured speech-therapy setting. The words, phrases, and sentences that were selected contained sibilant sounds in initial, medial, and final positions, and in blends. These are listed in Appendix II.

THE INSTRUCTIONAL SEQUENCE AND SYSTEM

The selection of materials was made by the clinician and T. W. She chose picture types from Mower's "S Pak" along with word lists and sentences from various sources such as Fairbanks's *Voice and Articulation Drill Book*. A series of 5″ × 8″ cards was devised for use in T. W.'s individualized instructional program.

Motivation to change the frontal lisp seemed to be at an extreme high just from the mere fact that the subject was to be a part of an experimental program or project. This acted as an intrinsic reward. In addition, T. W. chose a token system that she liked, as it was tangible: points evidenced by a system of colored chicken bands (plastic rings); upon receiving 200 points she would earn a reward of her choice. In advance, she had chosen a Dymo Labelett. A social reward of approval was given from the clinician. No negative reinforcement was used in the program.

Behavior Observed: Number of correctly produced sibilant sounds (/s/ and /z/) in contrast to the number of incorrectly produced sibilant sounds. Spontaneous speech that was tape-recorded and structured sentences containing /s/ and /z/ in all positions (initial, final, and medial) were utilized for the baseline. The recordngs were used as a check for correct tabulaton.

When Observed: During speech-therapy sessions 30 minutes in length, twice weekly, for a total of three hours. Dates of observation were March 8, March 10, March 15, March 17, March 22, and March 24, 1971.

Materials Used: Sentence list, Appendix I. Sony cassette tape recorder. Tabulation sheet with which check marks could be made beside correct and incorrect productions and then totaled at the end of each session.

Results: 54+ incorrectly produced sibilant sounds in contrast with 8 correctly produced sibilant sounds per session averaged for the entire three hours. This gave a ratio of 1.8/.26 incorrect over correct productions per 1-minute segment.

Observer: Susan Gilliland, speech pathologist.

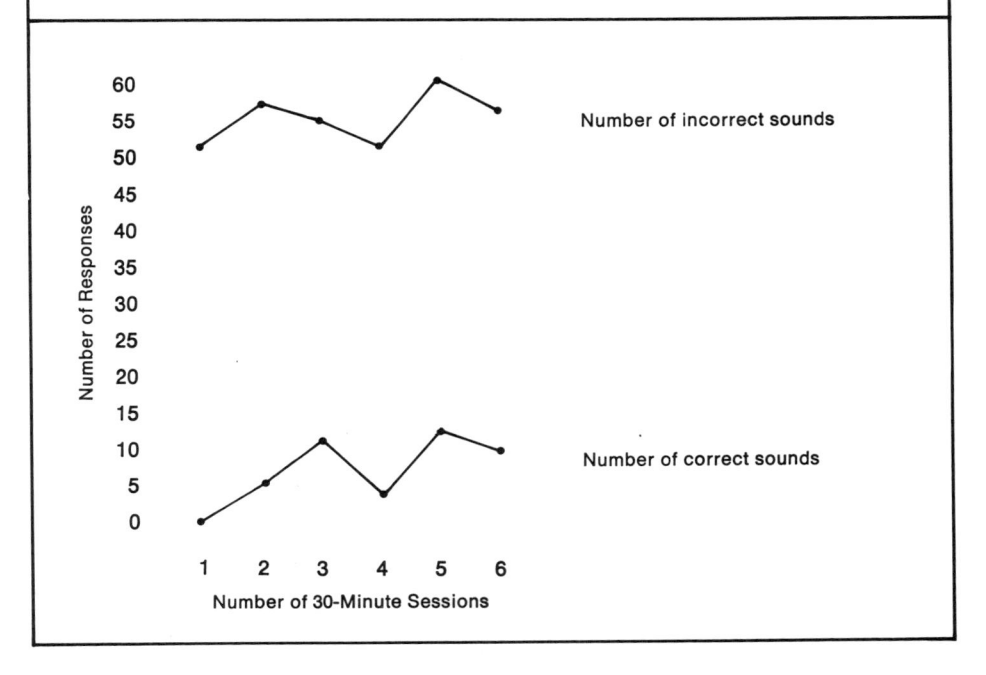

Figure 14. Baseline data, T.W.

A mixed-ratio reinforcement schedule that started with 100-percent reinforcement and diminished gradually to 20-percent reinforcement was utilized for T. W. For example, at first T. W. was awarded a band for every correct response, and later for every fifth correct response. Each new portion or new part of the program necessitated going back to the 100-percent reinforcement schedule with a gradual decline to 20 percent and then going back up again at the introduction of each new step.

The instruction program was administered to T. W. in a one-to-one structured speech-therapy situation. Only she and the clinician were present.

Mrs. W., the subject's mother, was consulted after the initial testing and evaluation period to set up a home program since T. W. was only to be seen one hour per week. She was shown, by video tape of an actual speech-therapy session, exactly what T. W. was doing that was incorrect, and then how T. W. produced correct /s/ and /z/ sounds. Mrs. W. was then asked to judge, with T. W. present, whether T. W. was making the correct or incorrect sound, and exactly what to do and say in the home program. The home-program booklet, with exact words to say and what responses to expect, was given to Mrs. W. with the remark that she would be called within the week to "see how things were going." This part of the program went so well that T. W. asked a sister to do some of the exercises with her and can do others alone in front of the mirror, with herself being the judge of whether she is correctly or incorrectly producing the sounds.

The instructional program was broken into a sequence of 14 individual parts. They are as follows:

1. Correct production and placement of the /s/ and /z/ sounds in isolation.
2. Correct production of initial /s/ and /z/ in syllables, words, and phrases.
3. Correct production of initial /s/ and /z/ in sentences. Correct production of initial /st/ and /sn/ in syllables, words, and phrases.
4. Correct production of initial /s/, /z/, /st/, /sn/ in sentences. Correct production of initial /sl/ and /sk/ in syllables, words, and phrases.
5. Correct production of initial /s/, /z/, /st/, /sn/, /sl/, and /sk/ in sentences. Correct production of initial /sp/, /sw/, and /sm/ in syllables, words, and phrases.
6. Correct production of all initial sibilant combinations in sentences. Correct production of the sounds /sh/, /zh/, /ch/, and /j/ in words, phrases, and sentences.
7. Correct production of final /s/ and /s/ in syllables, words, phrases, and short sentences.
8. Correct production of final /s/ and /z/ in more difficult sentences. Correct production of final /st/ and /sk/ in syllables, words, and phrases.
9. Correct production of final /s/, /z/, /st/, and /sk/ in sentences. Correct production of final /sp/, /sl/, /zl/, and /zm/ in syllables, words, and phrases.

10. Correct production of all final sibilants in sentences, paragraphs, and conversation.
11. Correct production of medial sibilants in words, phrases, and sentences.
12. Correct production of all sibilant sounds in sentences, paragraphs, and conversation.
13. Correct production of words containing difficult combinations of sibilant sounds. Correct production of these words in sentences, paragraphs, and conversation.
14. Correct production of all sibilant sounds in prepared paragraphs, chosen by student; sight reading, and conversation.

It should be said here that this is by no means a set program; it is highly individualized and was constructed, modified, and reconstructed to fit T. W. as the program progressed. This method of shaping through successive approximations led to a high and stable response of producing /s/ and /z/ sounds correctly 92 percent of the time in the structured speech-therapy situation.

Too, each time before a new step in the sequence was introduced, a criterion test was administered to determine if the subject was ready to move on to the next step. The success of the program is based on the mastery of each step before moving on to the next. In total there were fourteen criterion tests; five of these are listed in Appendix III.

RESULTS OF THE TREATMENT PROGRAM

The treatment program proved to be highly successful with T. W. The home program probably did as much for its success as the actual therapy sessions, if not more. This is probably due to the fact that T. W. was concerned with her speech in numerous situations other than the therapy situation, this concern prompting a quicker success in the program as a whole.

The treatment phase is added to the baseline information in the graph of Figure 15. Results of the treatment phase indicate an average of 92+ correctly produced sibilants in contrast with 7+ incorrectly produced sibilants for each thirty-minute session.

Some of the problems encountered through the use of this program were:

1. Is it necessary to use manipulable secondary reinforcers (chicken bands) that are external to the program instead of simple feedback in the way of knowledge of response correctness? The rewarding was a chore at times and quite awkward.
2. Is it critical that the subject be placed in a one-to-one relationship with the therapist for maximum success? It seems that efficiency is cut almost in half by placing more than one subject in a group.
3. Is there an advantage in having the speech therapist administer the program? Or could it be administered by any person able to make the judgments of right and wrong as to the particular problem involved?

4. Why is it not better to have a concentrated speech therapy program for a short period of time rather than an extended one in which the subject is seen only once or twice per week? It seems that justification of accountability could be seen through the number of successes and not the number of subjects seen. Is the emphasis in the wrong place?

The clinician felt that the program was well-suited to the subject. T. W. seemed to thrive on the successes she achieved in the few short sessions, although she admitted that she had used similar materials in previous therapy sessions without success.

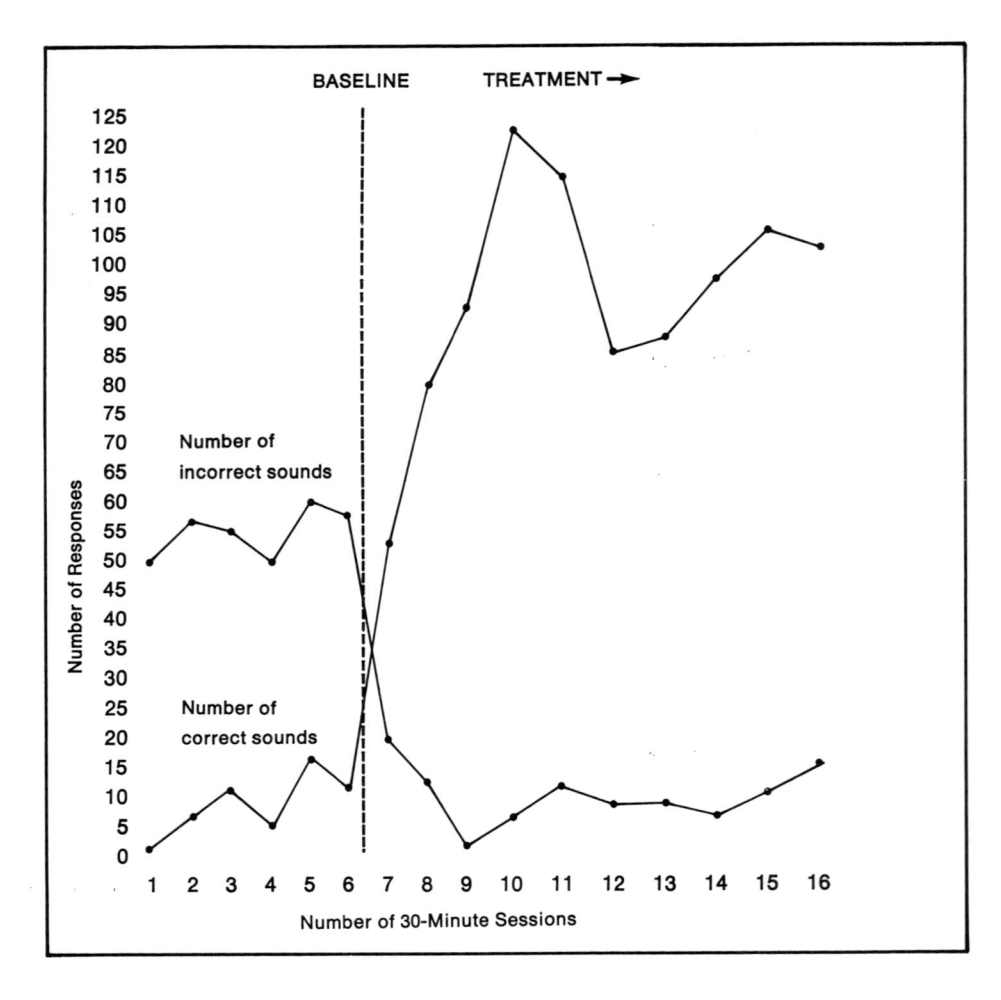

Figure 15. Baseline and treatment data, T.W.

FOLLOW-UP TO THE PROGRAM

By no means is T. W. ready for dismissal from speech therapy as "cured." Many programs seem to fall through because they are not taught with transfer in mind. Great care to teach for transfer must be included in the program. One cannot assume that the newly learned response will be used in daily speech after old errors have been reinforced in the same situation for years.

In T. W.'s program, a *transfer stage* must be included after the basic fourteen steps have stopped. This stage would involve a new setting, perhaps, or adding a person to the therapy session. Less structure to the therapy session would also be included in the transfer stage. A home setting, classroom setting, group setting, and others must be included for a complete and thorough transfer.

Then comes the *maintenance stage,* which involves periodic checks in the above situations to see if the corrected sibilant sounds are being maintained.

T. W.'s program will be carried on into the conversation area of step 12, where she is presently in the program. All fourteen steps should be established by the end of the school term in June, 1971. Her prognosis is good for continued success over the summer through the help of a well-planned home summer program.

APPENDIX I: PREPARED SENTENCES USED FOR TAPE-RECORDING THE SPEECH SAMPLE

1. Theater-goers always enjoy seeing *Alice in Wonderland.*
2. The sleeves in the coats and dresses are large this spring.
3. Psychology is one of the most interesting subjects studied in school.
4. Classes will be dismissed in a few days.
5. Have you had the pleasure of visiting the castle?
6. The beads scattered all over the classroom when the clasp of the chain broke.
7. The girls had just a smattering of French in school.
8. He swore on the Bible that what he said was true.
9. The sneak thief stole many costly jewels.
10. The date of Thanksgiving Day is set by annual proclamation of the President of the United States.
11. Sally's family always visits friends and relatives at the Christmas season.
12. Are you sure you can pronounce the sibilant sounds correctly in all cases?

NOTE: A different set of sentences was used for each session.

APPENDIX II. TARGET BEHAVIOR

Of the fifty responses that are listed below, forty-five are to be emitted correctly.

Words

solve	pencil	disk	dazzle	gossip
sought	zodiac	peace	cereal	wrist
psalm	sooth	loss	bustle	snake
chest	base	whistle	docile	does

Phrases

1. Scooping up a bucket of sand.
2. Sketching the view from the second-story window.
3. Sewing the sleeve.
4. Driving by a steel mill.
5. Sneering unkindly.
6. Sipping the tea.
7. Going to the zoo.
8. Buying a stamp.
9. Those are pearls.
10. The writer's design.
11. The farmer's wife.
12. Tickets for sale.
13. Sparkling water.
14. Western coast of California.
15. School superintendent.

Sentences

1. *Sense and Sensibility* was written by Jane Austen.
2. The assembly program will consist of extemporaneous speeches.
3. There are dozens of elastic bands on the second shelf.
4. We shall have celery soup and salmon sandwiches for lunch.
5. Please send several samples of silk at once.
6. He sang as he had never sung before.
7. "From the sublime to the ridiculous" is a trite expression.
8. There are poisonous snakes in those mountains.
9. After the sleet storm the trees were covered with ice.
10. The white fence was visible through the mist.
11. It does not seem possible that summer has come so soon.
12. Did James empty the wastepaper baskets Thursday?
13. This story ran in serial form in one of the magazines.
14. Sam has been seriously ill ever since Christmas.
15. This is the most unpleasant season of the year.

APPENDIX III. CRITERION TESTS

1. Say /s/ each time I nod my head. (five times)
   Say /z/ each time I nod my head. (five times)
2. Say the /s/ sound, combining it with these vowels: s-ah, s-ay, s-ee.
   Say the /z/ sound, combining it with these vowels: z-oh, z-oo, z-aw.
   Say these words after me: zeal, soon.
   Say these phrases: Sow the seed. Zero weather.
3. Repeat these after me: (a) Susan and her family lived in Seattle. (b) Did you see the zebra at the zoo?
   Say after me: steam, sneer, stumble, snore.
   Say these phrases: Taking a steamboat trip. Snipping the cloth.
   Say these phrases: Striking a snag. Making a statement.
4. Repeat these sentences after me: (a) The gardener said the ground was sandy. (b) The scene was weird at the zero hour. (c) Step right up to the front of the line. (d) The snow kept right on falling all night.
   Say after me: sleep, scold, sleeve, skull.
   Say these phrases: Scooping up a bucket of sand. Going for a sleigh ride.
5. Repeat these sentences after me: (a) The tired student stifled a yawn. (b) The farmer started to build a stone wall. (c) He slept right through the storm. (d) Don't sneer in public. (e) I seem to have forgotten his name. (f) What is your zodiac sign?
   Say after me: spelling, swan, smoke, smog.

The remaining criterion tests were constructed in much the same manner as tests 1-5.

CHAPTER 14

Task analysis and the development of social behavior: Peri

Peri is an 11½-year-old girl who is educationally handicapped because of negative self-concepts and resulting shyness, difficulty in expressing her emotions, and social-withdrawal tendencies. During a workshop on team approaches to diagnostic-prescriptive teaching, I presented a nine-step prescriptive programming procedure beginning with the "problem description" and ending with "program evaluation." This case illustrates the systematic use of task analysis and behavioral observation by a team which designs a program involving the total school. The team members who designed this program and wrote the report were Vernon Houser, learning-disabilities teacher; Kenneth W. Bohn, counselor; and H. Taylor-Godwin, school psychologist. This is a summary case study which illustrates how social and personal changes in a child's behavior may result from a relatively short period of prescriptive intervention.

DESCRIPTION OF SUBJECT

The following is a case description for "Peri," chosen as subject of the Prescriptive Teaching experiment. (Peri, a fictitious name derived from *exPERIment,* is used throughout this report.)

Peri is a Caucasian girl, 11½ years old, who is currently enrolled in a fifth-grade Educationally Handicapped Learning Disabilities Program. She lives with her father and mother, one older sister, age thirteen, two younger sisters, ages nine and five, and a younger brother, age seven. The father is a route salesman for a dairy company and the mother is a housewife. The family resides in a modest home in a housing tract of a generally middle-to-lower-middle-class neighborhood.

Peri's health history is not noteworthy, with the exceptions that her mother suffered a fall while in the seventh month of pregnancy, that Peri was born after three weeks of false labor, and that Peri had pneumonia at the age of four months. She is nearsighted and wears glasses.

Peri is very slow-moving. She tends to withdraw and is a loner who has few peer friends. She can read very well (in fact, uses reading as an escape mechanism), but does not achieve well in any other subject area. She is very dependent upon adults, does not like school, and has frequent stomachaches without apparent medical cause. Her rate of academic growth is generally declining.

Peri's older sister was born in a foreign country and was adopted while the father was assigned to that country during his service term. She is probably a gifted child, who learns rapidly and easily. It is believed that many of Peri's difficulties stem from the fact that she cannot meet the sister's competition academically.

Peri was enrolled in the special class in September 1970, and at the time the program experiment on prescriptive teaching began she had been in the program seven weeks.

DATA AND RECOMMENDATIONS

I. Problem Description

Social: Peri is a slow, quiet child whose behavior is introverted. She is too shy for a child her age. Her voice is often too low to understand. She offers nothing of her own in the classroom and shares none of her personal life or feelings with the class.

Academic: She applies herself only to those subjects she likes. She appears to use reading as an escape mechanism.

II. Objectives

Behavior Changes

	Increase	Decrease
Social	*Social interaction*—develop a friendship with one other girl. *Self-concept*—tell something satisfying from life once a week. *Physical Activities*—develop ability to play and enjoy one active game. *Expression of emotion*—express sadness or joy from a life situation independently once every two weeks. *Ability to communicate* (speak loudly).	Depression. Introversion. Vicarious involvement through reading. Dependence on adults.
Academic	Mathematics performance. Learn basic facts. Rename for subtraction. Learn concept of multiplication. Learn multiplication facts through 5's.	

III. Current Performance

Peri stands alone on the playground. She has to be asked to go out for recess. She shuns physical activities. Peri has been unable to make friends and is overly dependent on adults. When not supervised, she shifts from assignments to reading. Her reading and language areas are near grade level, but she has low mathematics skills. She is able to add and can carry three-place numbers, but does not know subtraction facts. She is unable to rename for subtraction and addition—her fact recall is slow. She often uses marks on her paper to complete problems. The reading problems in mathematics hold her interest for about ten minutes, but she cannot arrange such problems for solving.

IV. Present Program

Academic.
Teaching one-to-one ratio. Provided with own desk chalkboard. Personal comments. Praise. Written comments on paper. Drill using worksheets to improve subtraction skills. Combined pupil-teacher evaluation.

Social.
Set up interaction by working with a partner. Allow free talk during class time.

V. *Rewards.*

No extrinsic rewards except praise, written and oral comments.

VI. Strategy for Behavioral Change

Academic.
Use cash box and bundles of sticks to teach borrowing for subtraction.
Use number line to learn concept of multiplication.
Use *Language Master* cutout cards for mathematics facts.

Social.
Tutor younger child to increase self-concept.
Improve communication (speak loudly enough for a group to hear).
Use tape recorder to improve voice level.

VII. Parental Involvement

System of reward—see the parents.

VIII. Other Recommendations

Make a chart.
Use chart to win a party for the whole class—win approval and build self-concept.
Teachers to involve Peri in conversation.
Allow time to develop independence.

OUTCOMES

IX. Evaluation

On October 12, 1970, the program was begun, following the workshop. It was decided that we needed to develop another facet or two of Peri's personality.

After reviewing her files and her behavior, we felt Peri exhibited very little independence; therefore we began the program by developing a system of choices she must make. The tight structure of the classroom was reduced for a short period each day. Using this free time as a reward during the last twenty minutes of special-class instructional time proved gratifying. Suggestions were made that Peri could draw, work with students, use the filmstrip projector or the single-concept films. She was allowed to choose almost anything she wished except silent reading, since she used reading as an escape mechanism. At first, she interacted only with the one other girl in the group. She was transferred to another class period with a group of students among whom she was the only girl. Almost from the first day she used her superior skill of drawing at the board. This exhibition of skill seemed to increase her peer acceptance. After a few days she began reading filmstrips to small groups of boys who could not read but were interested in the subject.

Later, Peri was allowed time to help other students with spelling and language skills. The significant factor here was that she would read with a normal voice, whereas in the group reading previous to this her voice usually had been so low that only the teacher could understand her. She mentioned that she liked to read to other students.

Another facet of her personality appeared to be a general lack of emotion. During a conference with her, the teacher discussed feelings and emotions that a person feels at different times. Together, teacher and student developed a list of eight basic emotions such as happiness, sadness, worry, boredom. Following this, Peri removed pictures from magazines to portray these various emotions. She had no difficulty doing this, but lost interest before completing the notebook with the pictures. Other students then helped gather pictures, which Peri pasted in the book to finish the project. In every case she identified correctly the emotion that the group was trying to show with the pictures.

Following this, she read stories to the teacher and pointed out at given times how the person must have felt. We felt this helped her to feel more strongly about life situations.

Peri exhibited some weakness in the area of perceptual orientation. She had difficulty playing with much coordination or agility; for instance, when pitching ball she stepped out with the wrong foot. During class sessions, we worked on four-square, throwing and catching. It was felt she would use these skills on the playground, but after several days of practice, she still did not use the skills learned to play four-square. At the same time, however, she complained to her regular-class teacher that no one would play with her. His comment was "Have you asked anyone to play with you?" She said, "No, but I will try." From that time on she engaged constantly in handball and hopscotch. She has never played four-square, but she used her newly developed skills. On October 29 she was asked what her favorite game was. She answered, "I like several, but if you mean the best, hopscotch and handball."

Prior to the workshop, Peri's regular-class teacher stated she had no friends and did not play with anyone on the playground. Three weeks later, he felt Peri had changed remarkably. His report follows: "Peri used to stand in the middle of the hall so someone would notice her. When this didn't bring results, she would ask a safety patrolman to put her on the wall. This is a type of detention used by the safety patrol. The students who have to stand by the wall are given much attention. Periodically, they are told 'be quiet, don't move, stand straight,' etc. This seemed to satisfy Peri's need for attention." By early November, Peri had changed so much that she even talked out of turn in class. As she began to change she was put on the safety patrol and has done a capable job.

Academically, we gave attention to developing Peri's subtraction skills where renaming was involved. We started with boxes of coins from which she could make change. Following this, we used marks on the paper. She learned the concept rapidly. We made the subject somewhat easier for her to grasp by teaching her the additive method of subtraction. Peri disliked mathematics and still does. During the first month, especially, she would shift from mathematics to reading when working independently. She still will not work for long periods of time, but she can subtract even a complex problem accurately. The first month she spent ten minutes per day on the *Language Master,* using subtraction-fact cards with cutouts. After she started her answer, the correct answer was automatically given.

Peri has written several experience stories in which she has taken pictures from magazines, then made up a script to go along with the pictures. The first of these was about her cats. Another was about a trip to Mexico, where she rode her horses. Through these, we felt, she developed a small realization of her own potential. We felt that Peri has a great capacity for involvement, along with a sense of humor, which really hasn't surfaced yet.

Presently, we feel she has made great strides in several areas. She still dislikes mathematics but attacks mathematics language problems with a zeal and diligence totally lacking in arithmetic drill work.

Both teachers feel that her pattern of pleasing the teacher has evolved into one of independent behavior. We noticed that when teacher contact was reduced, it was immediately reflected in increased peer contact.

During Peri's last interview with the special-class teacher, she stated that this school was the best one she had ever attended. When questioned as to the reason, she replied, "Because the kids like me better. They are more friendly." The teacher asked, "Have you changed any?" to which Peri answered, "Yes, I've become less shy."

Although not yet finished, we have unleashed a wealth of individual potential. Peri sees herself as a more adequate person.

Peri's regular-class teacher has given much assistance by involving her in groups and providing praise and attention. He set up the party scheme that we suggested for outstanding work. This was our idea for developing in-group status and strengthening peer relations.

Peri's mother says Peri has improved 95 percent. During recent parent conferences, her father stated that Peri is a new person. We hope this enlightened view of home will be of valuable assistance for future development. Her parents feel they are more involved with her and will provide praise and encouragement.

CHAPTER 15

The learning resource center model

Diagnostic-prescriptive teachers traditionally work in schools, clinics, hospitals, and other institutional settings. In recent years a number of public-school districts have established unique community learning centers which are staffed in part by educational therapists and prescriptive specialists who supplement the efforts of the regular classroom teacher and special-education staff. The following report* of the Learning Resource Center for Exceptional Children (in the Sacramento City Unified School District) presents one model of supplementary services. Such a program is essential if diagnostic-prescriptive teaching is to become a reality with multihandicapped children and their families.

Although a variety of special education classes have been made available in most school districts, these have usually been limited and have not been sufficient to meet the needs of the pupils. For instance, special educators have recognized the importance of providing individualized instruction, proper programing, consultant help in curriculum development, and continued inservice training. The need to provide for multiply handicapped pupils and those requiring special educational therapy or counseling has also been recognized, but seldom met. Similarly, parent participation, counseling, and education have been identified as a necessary part of the educational process although such programs have seldom been given much priority.

THE LEARNING RESOURCE CENTER

In the spring of 1968 the Sacramento City Unified School District was awarded funds under Title VI of the Elementary and Secondary Education Act to establish a Learning Resource Center for Exceptional Children with the primary objective of stimulating the development of prescriptive teaching approaches by providing supplemental services to the regular special education program. No attempt was made to provide additional classes for exceptional children. Emphasis was placed on the development of resource services in the areas of psychoeducational evaluation and programing, educational therapy, pupil and parent counseling, inservice training, and parent education. Priority was given to multiply handicapped pupils with significant learning disabilities for whom the existing educational program was inadequate.

*Reprinted with permission. "The Learning Resource Center for Exceptional Children," *Exceptional Children*, Vol. 36, No. 7 (March, 1970), pp. 527–530.

STAFF AND FACILITIES

The staff of the Learning Resource Center consists of four professionals and two secretaries. A psychoeducational specialist is the director and consulting psychologist for the staff, parents, and teachers involved. An educational therapist provides direct therapy for a number of children who come to the center on an appointment basis. The educational psychologist assists teachers in educational programing and planning classroom pilot projects, conducts special evaluations, and works with parent groups. A demonstration teacher helps teachers develop exemplary programs and works with selected children upon assignment. All four members of the team work directly with pupils in some continuing capacity. In addition to the center staff, seven school psychologists and three program coordinators (for the physically handicapped, educationally handicapped, and mentally retarded) serve special education teachers and are involved in consultation and the screening of referrals.

The Learning Resource Center is located in the wing of a regular elementary school. One room, equipped with an observation window and a sound recording system, is the psychoeducational clinic for task analysis of motor and perceptual skills and related learning disabilities. The adjacent room is used for educational therapy and is equipped with educational materials and programing aids. The third room is the resource training room and houses conference tables for inservice training, parent education, and educational materials classified by specific learning disabilities.

PSYCHOLOGICAL EVALUATION AND PROGRAMING

The goal of the Learning Resource Center staff is to provide specific consulting services to teachers, coordinators, and psychologists. When the center receives a request for help in developing an effective special education program for an individual pupil and his parents, the center personnel may meet with the requesting school's staff to review the problem and cooperatively plan a number of positive interventions. These interventions usually include the individualization of the program with special materials, flexible scheduling, behavior modification, parent involvement, and the planning of classroom strategies.

The center also has consulting sessions where teachers and psychologists come to the center to discuss selected cases, to request help in designing special projects, or to confer on educational problems. An example of this approach would be a staff meeting, including the parents, to devise a cooperative home and school behavior modification program for a disturbed boy.

In most cases in which children are referred to the center considerable psychological and related information is already available. The usual initial procedure is to make some developmental task analysis of functional performance in gross motor, sensory motor, perceptual, language, conceptual, and social skill areas (Valett, 1967) in order to select appropriate tasks and thus create an effective program allowing the child to function in some school setting. For example, a six year old, deaf, blind, and mildly retarded child was successfully, but gradually, programed into special education following task analysis and prescriptive programing.

EDUCATIONAL THERAPY

The educational therapy program began with several severely handicapped pupils who had been exempted from school attendance. Following task analysis and evaluation of each child's basic learning abilities with specially developed instruments (Valett, 1966, 1968), individualized therapy programs were developed. Special emphasis was placed on programing specific motor, perceptual, language, and cognitive abilities with parental involvement. Parents first viewed their children through the observation window; gradually, they participated directly in the therapy room and were expected to follow up on home assignments with special prescriptions for learning (Valett, 1970) as specified by the assigned therapist. During the year, 21 children, their parents, and all the staff members worked on this basis.

Educational therapy is supplemental to regular special education placement. However, due to the extent of their disability, eight children continued in intensive therapy three to five sessions per week without school placement. The major problem continues to be effective liaison with special class teachers so that the pupil can continue in the class, or return to it as soon as possible, while receiving the essential supporting help.

The center operates a small activity group for teaching children basic socialization skills prior to integration into special classes. The group is conducted twice a week under the leadership of the demonstration teacher, with parents participating on a regularly assigned basis.

PARENT AND PUPIL COUNSELING

A number of parents of exceptional children have requested counseling or consulting services for themselves or their children. As a result of a brochure sent to parents describing the services of the center, many requests for special help were received. Of these requests, 28 were given to consulting school psychologists and program coordinators who then worked with the pupils and parents concerned.

An additional 17 parents were seen at the center for special counseling and programing. In most cases several sessions were held with each parent to help each one define and cope with the problems of his exceptional child. Typical cases consisted of helping parents select and modify specific child behaviors, such as aggression, which were upsetting both at home and in school; many other sessions focused on parental concerns in dealing with enuresis and self help skills.

Although most pupil counseling is conducted by the special education teachers and school counselors or psychologists, occasional help is requested from the center. Cases, such as working with a boy with suicidal inclinations or with a child who has repeatedly run away from home, involve close liaison with the referring teacher or psychologist. During the year, seven pupils were seen for this kind of supportive counseling.

PARENT EDUCATION

One of the most exciting and successful programs offered by the center has been parent education. At the beginning of the school year, announcements were sent out that interested parents could register for 10 week courses on understanding and managing children's behavior problems. Both morning and evening sessions were offered under the leadership of the educational psychologist and the psychoeducational specialist. Semiprogramed lessons (Patterson and Gullion, 1968; Valett, 1969a) and other materials which were used covered such subjects as establishing objectives, teaching desirable behavior, using reinforcement, and managing special problems.

Throughout the year four classes and three followup discussion groups were held with 93 parents participating. Classes usually began with the instructor's introducing the topic. Then lesson materials for parents to work on in the class were distributed, and the subsequent discussion centered around selected problems or concerns relevant to the topic. "Homework" consisted of projects requiring systematic observation of children, selection and modification of target behaviors, and the development of reward and recording systems. Parents then brought their projects to class for a discussion of their approaches to a problem. Approximately 75 percent of the parents who began the classes finished and reported positive results in modifying their children's behavior.

Seventy-nine percent of the parents reported that the classes were of "very much" or "much" help in teaching them how to understand and manage their children's behavior; other responses were "average" (12 percent), "little help" (7 percent), and "very little help" (2 percent). Some other significant responses were the following: 94 percent felt the course material and topics to be "very good" or "good" while 93 percent found the class discussions "very helpful" or "helpful." Numerous statements were also received of which the following are typical:

> It taught us how to observe and where to start in trying to modify our boy's behavior. The specific directions were most helpful.

> It helped me to find a more positive and effective way of dealing with my child, and in that way to really enjoy him more. It showed me that parents first must change their attitude before they can help their children overcome behavior problems.

> It gave me a completely new approach to controlling our kids.

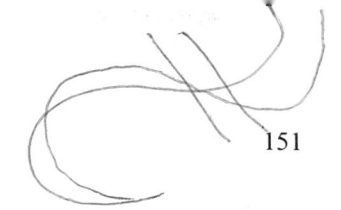

Suggestions from parents for improving the course included longer class periods, more audiovisual materials, specialized classes for parents of teenagers, more followup classes, and more provision for individual counseling of parents.

INSERVICE TRAINING

A major function of the Learning Resource Center has been to provide resources and training programs for special education personnel. The resource training room and the demonstration teacher have served as the focal points of this program, although all staff members have been involved. Many different inservice training programs and services were made available including the following:

1. A preschool workshop on prescriptive teaching for 14 selected teachers and special educators was held.
2. A preschool workshop on prescriptive planning in special education for 23 administrators, psychologists, and program coordinators was held.
3. Special group meetings were conducted with 162 special education teachers introducing them to program materials available through the center.
4. New materials (over 790 items) were checked out for use by special education teachers.
5. More than 300 teachers, college students, and out of district persons visited the resource training room for help in program development.
6. Demonstration teacher services were provided upon request to 30 special education teachers.
7. A 17 week two unit salary credit course on behavior modification and task analysis in special education for 19 teachers interested in developing prescriptive teaching programs with their own classrooms was offered.

Future plans include extending inservice credit courses to cover specialized courses for secondary teachers and additional prescriptive teaching courses for new elementary special educators. Demonstration teacher services will be extended to permit large blocks of time (up to a month or more) to be spent assisting interested teachers in developing model classrooms.

IMPLICATIONS

On the basis of experience to date, several major program implications warrant careful consideration.

Parent education should receive priority and should be rapidly extended. Emphasis should be placed on the early involvement of parents in parent education and participation programs. Programs should be available to all parents of referred children with learning or behavioral problems.

More attention should be given to early consultation with teachers concerned with learning problems by encouraging teachers to request consultation on exceptional children and their programs early in the school year. A more intensive followup service, which may require the psychologist or other specialist to spend a number of consecutive days in a classroom to work through a given problem, should be provided.

Educational therapy is an additional resource program and does not replace the ongoing special education class. All exceptional children should have some group or class placement. Since it is difficult to bridge the gap between individual educational therapy and the more usual special education program, a number of varied level activity groups for multiply handicapped children could be used as a stepping stone to the usual special program. Since educational therapy should be viewed as a temporary resource, it should be provided on a contract basis to the children of parents who agree to become directly involved in home training and parent education. Educational therapy needs to be continued in the summer if these handicapped children are to retain the gains made during the school year.

Learning Resource Center counseling services should continue to emphasize behavior modification and short term involvement. Conjoint family counseling and group counseling should be developed. Parent and adolescent groups should be continuous to allow group placement of exceptional children and/or their parents when necessary. With the participation of district counselors and psychologists in specialized counseling groups such a situation would be feasible.

The inservice training program has been particularly effective in stimulating innovative practices, since teachers have participated voluntarily in special classes. Summer workshops should also be developed as an extended part of inservice training with priority given to new teachers. Demonstration teacher effectiveness can be enhanced through longer assignments to teachers interested in working on classroom planning and organization problems.

REFERENCES

Patterson, G., and M. E. Gullion. *Living with Children.* Champaign, Ill.: Research Press, 1968.

Valett, Robert E. *Modifying Children's Behavior.* Belmont, Calif.: Fearon Publishers, 1969.

———. *Prescriptions for Learning.* Belmont, Calif.: Fearon Publishers, 1970.

———. *The Psychoeducational Inventory.* Belmont, Calif.: Fearon Publishers, 1968.

———. *The Remediation of Learning Disabilities.* Belmont, Calif.: Fearon Publishers, 1967.

———. *The Valett Developmental Survey of Basic Learning Abilities.* Palo Alto, Calif.: Consulting Psychologists Press, 1966.

CHAPTER 16

Using the learning resource center: Beverly

Beverly is a brain-damaged girl age eight years seven months, who required the supplementary services of the Learning Resource Center. Following an automobile accident, Beverly could no longer cope with the demands of the regular classroom. Upon leaving the hospital she began to receive educational therapy in the Resource Center for approximately forty-five minutes a session on an appointment schedule. Over sixty individual prescriptive-teaching sessions plus twenty-two group-activity sessions were provided over a six-month period before she was ready to be reintroduced to a formal school program. Then she was gradually integrated into a special education class for the educable mentally retarded, where she adapted very well. This case illustrates the importance of involving parents in home training programs and the necessity for a cooperative team approach in the education of multihandicapped children.

PSYCHOEDUCATIONAL REPORT

Name: Beverly T.
Address: 675 Mora Way
Parents: Mr. and Mrs. A.T.
Referred by: Mr. Sam Ellis, Principal

Date of report: May 16, 1969
Birthdate: 10-4-60
Chronological age: 8-7
School: Jefferson School

Reason for the Referral: Psychoeducational evaluation, programming, and educational therapy.

Evaluation procedures:
- Systematic observations from January 3, 1969, to present time.
- Vineland Social Maturity Scale.
- Stanford-Binet L-M.
- Valett Developmental Survey of Basic Learning Abilities.
- Gesell Index of Maturation.
- Peabody Picture Vocabulary Test, Form A.

History

Beverly was referred to the Learning Resource Center on December 16, 1968, by Mr. Ellis, principal of Jefferson Elementary School, where Beverly had been attending the regular program. School reports had rated her "excellent" in physical education and art with reading on Level IV; she was a good student, independent and responsible in completing assignments; records also indicate her limitations had been in arithmetic and "talks too much." On September 28, 1968, Beverly was involved in an automobile accident resulting in a severe laceration of the leg. While in the hospital and following the administration of Xylocain for a wound on her left lower extremity, she developed a seizure and became comatose for some time. Upon her regaining consciousness it was apparent that she had regressed developmentally. She was then referred to the Rand Speech and Hearing Center for speech therapy and subsequently to the Learning Resource Center for Exceptional Children, as regular school placement was no longer possible.

A report from Mr. J., speech pathologist at Rand Community Hospital, dated March 31, 1969, carried the diagnosis of dysphasia characterized by both receptive and expressive disorders. Verbal responses were echoic or limited to simple expressions. She was then seen several times a week in 30-minute sessions with very slow progress and a guarded prognosis. She was referred to this Center for special training, and speech therapy was then discontinued.

Initial Evaluation

Mrs. T. was first seen on December 30, 1968. She described Beverly as having "extensive brain damage" with distorted speech and poor recognition of people and places. The *Vineland Social Maturity Scale* resulted in a social age of 4-4 years. Beverly was then seen on January 3, 1969, and appeared outgoing, relaxed, highly interested and curious; distractibility was obvious and there was an absence of integrated speech. Gross motor skills appeared fairly intact although she was confused over some body parts and space orientation; there was poor balance and confused laterality, directionality, and time orientation. In the perceptual areas, her receptive language was confused, with poor visual coordination and very limited visual-motor skills. At that time she did respond to the *Binet* on the two-year level although she was unable to complete the four-block tower. At Year II-6 she could identify all parts of the body but failed or rejected all other tasks. However, she was able to respond to a number of four-year items on the Developmental Survey, including color and number concepts and some language items (for instance, "brother is a boy, sister is a: *girl*";) ("father is a man, mother is a: *lady*"). One week later, Beverly was examined by Dr. Z. through private arrangements, and attained a *Vineland* social age of 4-3 and a *Binet* mental age of 3.2 with an intelligence quotient of 32. Dr. Z. also noted that she was very limited in her responses, with short interest and attention span, and easily upset.

Educational Therapy

Priority was given to establishing a training routine both in the Center and at home whereby Beverly could learn to attend and develop self-control. The parents were given lessons on home management and the training of children with behavior problems and were urged to join a parent education group concerned with these problems. However, the parents did *not* join the group and proved very inconsistent and unreliable in working with Beverly at home.

Arrangements were made to see Beverly in educational therapy for three thirty-minute sessions per week. The beginning program focused on gross motor activities such as crawling, jumping, and throwing, together with visual-motor activities including basic form-board manipulations, picture-puzzle integration, and bead-pattern stringing. Auditory-vocal-association activities were also programmed using EFI audio-cards (Electronic Futures Incorporated) whereby Beverly would listen and name basic sounds. The home training program consisted of jogging, jumping, crawling, tracing basic design templates, puzzle manipulation, body balance, cutting, and simple visual-matching activities. Operant conditioning was used in both the Center and home program with candy, food, and surprise gifts as rewards.

When Beverly began the program in January, there was much balking and almost constant negativism expressed although most of the time she completed her tasks. A systematic approach with intermittent rewards proved effective in motivating her to attend and respond. Progress was noted shortly in body control, form-board completion, cutting, and matching activities. Fine muscle coordination, as in beading and pencil control, was longer in developing. Following two months of intensive work, a home call disclosed great inconsistency on the parents' part which seemed to be negating much of the work done in the Center. It was then decided that one parent would have to be present during the therapy period to assist in working with Beverly and to train the parents in how to follow through at home. Since that time, both parents have participated in educational therapy although the nurse is now bringing Beverly and works with her both here and at home. Significant progress has been made with home training, now including alphabet matching, tracing, advanced puzzle work, and selected home chores to develop cooperation and responsibility.

For the last month more demands have been made of Beverly in educational therapy. These have included work with seventeen-piece puzzles, tracing basic forms and alphabet letters, tracing letter symbols in the "Write and See" Book 1, matching alphabet cards, and completing alphabet-picture puzzle cards. In addition Beverly has been brought into the activity group, which meets twice weekly for forty-five minutes, where emphasis is placed on cooperative play and socialization.

Current Evaluation and Impressions

This girl has made significant gains over the past five months with progress most noticeable in expressive language, visual-motor control, and visual matching.

LEARNING RESOURCE CENTER FOR EXCEPTIONAL CHILDREN · EDUCATIONAL THERAPY PLAN

Pupil's name *Beverly T.* Date: Beginning *Feb. 11* Ending *March 11*

OBJECTIVE Sequential Behavior Goals	LESSON PLAN Teaching Strategy and Time Allocations	LESSON MATERIALS Aids and Test Assignments	PUPIL RESPONSE Performance Record (VW 0, W 1, A 2, S 3, VS 4) 2/11	2/13	2/14	2/18	2/19	2/20	2/21	2/26	2/27	2/28	3/4	3/11
Crawling	Under chairs and around Kiddie Cayuse and return	Chairs; Cayuse	2	2	2	3	3	2	3	3	-	3		
Jumping	Over balance beam	Beam	2	2	2	3	3	3	2	3	-			
	Rope forward	Rope tied to Cayuse	0	1	2	3	3	3	2	3	-	3		
Small-muscle coordination	Replace mixed shapes in slots	Sequence form board	3+	3	3	3	3	3	3	3	4	4	4	4
	Complete puzzles: Rooster	Rooster	2	2	2	2	2	2		2+				
	Complete puzzles: Duck								2+		3	3	4	3
	Trace small stencils and cut out strips	Basic form Template	1	1	1+	2	2	2	3	-	2	2	4	3
		Scissors; stencil	1						2					
Auditory-vocal association	Identify sounds by sentences: "That is a ______"	EFI cards: Set 1, Cards C1-C15, A1-A12	2	2	3	3		2	2	3	-	3	3	
Small-muscle coordination; finger dexterity; visual matching	Duplicate bead pattern	Small colored beads	2	2	2	-	2+	2	3	-	3	3	3+	
Spatial relationships	Duplicate domino-block designs	Domino blocks	2	2	3	-			3	-	-			
Throwing	Across table to clown	Bean-bag throw				-				-	-			
Handwriting	Hand control	Handwriting with Write and See				1	1	1	0		-			

EVALUATION AND COMMENT

- 2/11 Cannot rotate puzzles. Drops beads. Places blocks so they fall off table
- 2/14 Jump rope 5X. Used complete sentence with EFI. Block train on floor.
- 2/18 more alert. Does not rotate. Handwriting with "Write and See".
- 2/20 Balked
- 2/25 much better v-m coordination although more negative and rejecting.
- 2/27 Introduced Bev. and mother to Mrs Jones and to motor-room activities. Mrs. Jones showed tasks performed. Good motivation today
- 2/28 Good response
- 3/4 Good verbal response. Excellent use of basic form stencil. Also used extended Survey task items.
- 3/11 Balked and rejected many tasks; negativistic.

Figure 16.

She now cuts on line patterns and has improved her attention span although her frustration tolerance remains very limited. Although she has been on medication, her parents have reported they are very erratic in giving it to her and a question exists as to whether improved attention and a further reduction in hyperactivity would result from reevaluation of medication. Beverly remains a very moody and erratic child and considerable work needs to be done in behavior modification involving the parents. During the week of May 12 some standardized reevaluation was made. At this time she was able to complete a circle, a cross, and a partial square with a corresponding visual-motor age of 4½ years on the *Gesell Index of Maturation;* this is progress over the original scribble stage. With the nurse as informant, her *Vineland social age* is 5-3 with a corresponding social quotient between 60 and 65, specific gains being reported in self-help skills such as bathing, using a knife at the table, skating, dressing, and toilet care. On the *Binet* her receptive vocabulary improved from the two-year to the four-year level, which was her greatest gain. In a similar way, her bead-stringing performance (thirteen in two minutes) is on the 4½-year level but with other erratic and scattered performance skills down to the three-year age level. Correspondingly good responses were obtained on the *Peabody Picture Vocabulary Test* with an earned mental age of four years seven months and an intelligence quotient (receptive language) of 58.

There is no question but that Beverly remains a moderately mentally retarded child with significant brain damage that has affected both her functional intelligence and personality. She has proven educable, however, and will continue to need special education throughout her life. Although progress will be slow, she will continue to make significant gains with special training and therapy.

Recommendations

1. Beverly should be placed in the primary educable-mentally-retarded class for behaviorally disturbed children in the Harrison School. She should begin the class in September on a one-hour modified day to start.

2. Her educational program should consist of much structure with the use of tangible rewards (including stars and access to selected toys such as "Play-Doh"—which is highly motivating to her).

3. Programming should continue with alphabet matching, tracing activities including Frostig materials, expressive language lessons (Peabody, etc.), and continued use of "Write and See" materials.

4. Supplementary educational therapy on a once- or twice-a-week basis should be provided by the Learning Resource Center with transfer to classroom activities.

5. The possibility of further medical review and management (through such drugs as Ritalin, etc.) will be requested of her physician.

6. The parents should be seen on a regular consultation basis through the Learning Resource Center to continue the home training program and to become further involved in parent education.

7. Over the summer the parents should enroll Beverly in the Easter Seal swimming and special summer program if at all possible.

As the psychoeducational management of this child will continue to pose difficult problems, occasional case-review meetings involving all concerned should be held at the Learning Resource Center.

PUPIL PROGRESS REPORT

This report on Beverly was prepared by the psychoeducational specialist at the Learning Resource Center, using a form usually completed by the child's classroom teacher at the end of each school semester. It is dated June 11, 1969.

Gross Motor Development (programs and progress in motor activities, physical education, general health, etc.): Beverly has progressed through obstacle-crawling, throwing, and jumping activities. Improvement has been made in all areas, with better coordination. The home program still includes sit-ups and jumping jacks.

Sensory-Motor Integration (programs and progress in motor integration, art, music, etc.): Much difficulty here. Future program should include eurhythmics and art activities.

Perceptual-Motor Skills (programs and progress in perceptual skills including listening, attention and memory, fine muscle coordination): Great progress made. In January Beverly could not replace simple puzzle forms, follow a bead pattern, trace designs, or cut a line. She now has good visual matching and her visual-motor coordination is much improved.

Language (programs and progress in language usage, including functional level of reading, writing, and spelling): Expressive language has gradually developed. She is using sentences and can sequence some nursery rhymes. For the last six weeks she has been working on the alphabet with touch cards and wooden letters and now identifies *a, b, c, e, i, j, k, l, m, o, p, r, t, u, v, w,* and *z.*

Conceptual Skills (programs and progress in arithmetic understanding, social studies, fund of information, concept development): Few number concepts although she can group simple sets and count objects to twenty without confusion. She needs training in simple classifications and comprehension skills.

Social Skills (programs and progress in social and personal development, including self-control, responsibility, and general behavior): Beverly now follows directions, cooperates in the activity group, and has learned to control much of her behavior. However, she can quickly become negativistic.

General Comments: Beverly began educational therapy on 1-9-69 and continued through 6-10-69 averaging three individual sessions and two group activity sessions per week.

What recommendations do you have regarding educational placement and progress for this pupil for the forthcoming semester or year? Educable-mentally-retarded primary class at the Harrison School in September 1969. The attached home training program was recommended to the parents for the summer months.

Anecdotal Notes

This portion of the Pupil Progress Report is a selection of anecdotal notes from the initial six months' prescriptive-education program in the Learning Resource Center.

1-3-69: Very distractible, no integrated speech, poor balance, much auditory confusion. Total inability to match simple wooden basic designs.

2-11-69: Cannot rotate or complete simple six-piece puzzles; places kindergarten blocks so they fall off table.

2-25-69: Somewhat better visual-motor coordination although highly negative and rejecting of tasks.

3-4-69: Good verbal responses—intact and understandable. Good use of basic-form stencils for tracing.

3-24-69: Began tactile training for language expression. Was able to match simple letters, numbers, and words.

4-8-69: Introduced Playskool occupational-concept matching cards. She did quite well on the first six presented.

4-21-69: Notable improvement in gross motor coordination. Copied all basic designs for first time with some success.

5-9-69: Very cooperative today. A high response rate of 65 tasks completed. Did well on the seventeen-piece goose puzzle. Also enjoyed matching alphabet cards with moderate success. Good results in cutting paper on lines. Home training program is reported as going very well.

5-20-69: Initially negative but then responded quite well to a number of modified tasks such as stringing bead patterns.

5-26-69: Responded well to alphabet matching and oral letter identification.

6-2-69: Began 19-piece puzzle. Also started EFI rhymes with much interest.

6-9-69: Was initially negative but finally made 125 responses. Mother was present and is now positive and rewarding. Beverly matched wooden letters and did fairly well on simple rhymes.

Recommended 1969 Summer Home Training Program

1. **Art activities:** Cut and paste. Finger paint. Easel tempera painting.
2. **Continue puzzles:** 20-24 pieces.
3. **Sort and trace alphabet letters.**
4. **Copy alphabet letters on lined paper.**
5. Group simple sets and count things.
6. Skip, swim, jump rope.
7. Work on letter sounds and associations (phonic rummy).

Obtain educational games and toys as checked on accompanying sheets and make them available for free play as well as for home training sessions.

DEMONSTRATION TEACHER'S REPORT

The following report, dated June 10, 1969, was supplied by Mrs. Jones, to whom Beverly and her mother were introduced on February 27.

Beverly participated in the Group Activity for twenty-two sessions. The activities consisted of music, gross motor activities, and arts and crafts. Beverly's behavior improved a great deal and she responded to all activities. She was willing to attempt to do any task given to her. At times she showed aggressive behavior. However, it lasted for only a few minutes. She was very active at all times.

Beverly's attention span increased from three to fifteen minutes, or more, and by the end of the session she was beginning to be a real leader. She responds well to the various reinforcers. Beverly enjoyed all motor activities and singing. She could remember most of the songs and actions. The nurse stated that she always looked forward to coming in for the activities. The parent or nurse participated in the group activity with Beverly.

CHAPTER 17

The evaluation and development of basic learning abilities: Billy

The use of standardized intelligence tests as diagnostic-prescriptive instruments for the categorizing and placement of children in public-school programs is now under widespread attack. Although teachers rarely administer individual tests of general intelligence, they often give group tests of mental ability. Most diagnostic-prescriptive teachers do attempt to use the results of intelligence tests in developing educational prescriptions. Some of the issues involved are discussed in this final chapter, which was presented as an invited address to teachers of exceptional children. The case of Billy J. is incorporated as an illustration of the primary importance of the developmental task approach, rather than intelligence testing, in the functional diagnosis and educational prescription for children with learning and behavioral difficulties.

The school psychologist is currently involved in the dilemma of how to use intelligence tests appropriately in his professional practice. Although many state laws stipulate the use of individual intelligence tests, in the identification and classification of the "educable" and "trainable mentally retarded" child, for example, the way such tests are being used is causing the public and profession alike to reevaluate both use and function.

The debate has recently intensified, with attacks upon the misuse of I.Q. scores by teachers, as a result of Rosenthal's and Jackson's report (1969) that teacher expectancy based on I.Q. scores becomes an apparent determiner of pupil performance in the classroom. In addition, the placement of children in segregated classes for "special education" on the basis of I.Q. scores has been castigated by Dunn (1968) and other prominent special educators. However, it appears that the recent attacks by militant minority groups on the use of intelligence tests and the increasing number of legal suits against local school districts for alleged misplacement of children in special education classes are the prime movers resulting in the reappraisal of psychometric practices and priorities.

It was my privilege to deliver the keynote address at the annual convention of the Illinois Council for Exceptional Children in Chicago on October 28, 1971. This address, which forms the text of this chapter, was published in an abridged version as "Developmental Task Analysis and Psychoeducational Programming" in *Journal of School Psychology*, Vol. 10, No. 2. The *Journal* has given permission to reprint its version.

Should intelligence testing be abandoned by the school psychologist? Or should a moratorium on its use be applied until the use of tests is more strictly controlled? And what direction might the profession provide to its practitioners if existing testing practices are to be set aside? These are but a few of the related questions that demand response and widespread debate by all concerned.

WHAT IS BEING TESTED?

As far back as 1799 we have detailed records of the intellectual assessment of a "mentally retarded" child; this excellent report is the well-known *Wild Boy of Aveyron* by Itard. To my knowledge this is the earliest attempt to relate intellectual evaluation procedures to the direct instruction of the child. Today this would be recognized as developmental task analysis for the purpose of providing specific prescriptive instruction to Victor, the "wild boy." I will never forget the thrill I experienced years ago upon first reading this exciting account of an attempt to appraise and develop specific intellectual and behavioral abilities in such a child. Itard fully realized the necessity to break intelligence into its functional components for educational purposes, and this effort continues to offer an outstanding model for the practicing school psychologist today. What in fact was being evaluated was a number of sensory, language, cognitive, and social skills—or basic learning abilities—the combination of which eventuated in the formulation of specific educational objectives and instructional strategies.

Since then, others have taken the same approach. In 1883, G. Stanley Hall emphasized the importance of determining the developmental level of the child and of prescribing his education accordingly; he also recognized the many facets of intelligence, as evidenced by statements like ". . . a few days in the country [for the child] at this age has raised the level of many a city child's intelligence more than a term or two of school training could do without it" (quoted in McCullers, 1969). Certainly, Hall recognized that "intelligence" was influenced by the growth experiences of education and environmental expectation and that one of the purposes of education should be the enhancement of these basic learning abilities. Binet recognized the dynamic character of intelligence and pointed out that judgment, reasoning, initiative, and invention were components requiring careful attention (Binet and Simon, 1916). Although the multifactor nature of environmental problem solving was recognized by the early psychologists, the tendency of applied psychometrists was to interpret the Binet scale and other single-quotient scores as fixed indicators not subject to modification. This has been extremely unfortunate in that the reaction was bound to be rejection of the I.Q. score as an adequate means by itself for programming strategies to change human behavior. A few years ago Quinn McNemar reviewed the many reasons presented for discarding the idea of general intelligence and concluded with ". . . the hope that the I.Q. is replaced by something better rather than something worse" (McNemar, 1964).

The possibility of finding "something better" by concentrating on the individual's "style" of problem-solving and the analysis of developmental tasks and growth stages has been studied by Piaget for years. The dynamic processes of intellectual growth have now been described in detail (Piaget, 1952) and have helped contribute to the revolution in the assessment and concomitant education of children. Dissatisfaction with the single I.Q. score also prompted many other investigators to search for varied abilities and to devise multifactor approaches to measurement; certainly one of the more successful psychologists in this regard has been J. P. Guilford, who concluded that "exercise appropriate to each intellectual ability is likely to promote increase in that ability" (Guilford, 1967). A continuing problem, of course, has stemmed from the findings of recognized research that most of what we call intelligence or basic ability seems to be attributable to genetic factors (Burt, 1958), although it is also widely recognized that "innate ability" can be shaped by education and environmental modifiers and is not always reliably represented by I.Q. scores. This fact has recently been brought to the attention of many lawmaking bodies throughout the country, as in the requested report to the California State Legislature (California State Department of Education, 1970), which states that ". . . I.Q. scores may be useful in predicting academic success and demonstrating mastery of certain information or skills correlated with academic aptitude; however, they are not necessarily adequate measures of intelligence per se." The same report concludes that tests should result in more descriptive terms useful for educational purposes and that a "learning assistance program" should then be devised for all children in need, which would replace the present categorical system of special education.

Thus psychologists have long been aware of the limitations of single-test scores such as I.Q.'s and have openly stated their reservations to the public. At the same time the profession has continued to insist that psychoeducational assessment is an essential but preliminary step in the total evaluation of these basic learning abilities and of subsequent educational planning for their development. The problem facing such practitioners as the school psychologist is how to ethically use single-test scores such as I.Q.'s, while recognizing that they are but a small although significant *part* of the professional evaluation procedure. A concomitant part of the same problem is the selection of other means of evaluating the basic learning abilities which may have more relevance to the educational development of these same abilities and skills. While the profession has been wrestling with these questions for some time, it is now evident that increasing public pressures are expediting this change in emphasis.

SOME PUBLIC DEMANDS

Journalists, civic organizations, and various investigators have long championed the rights of the individual in this country. They have been careful watchdogs of our institutions (including professional organizations) to insure against unjust actions such as arbitrary institutionalization, segregation, or "placement" of the citizenry. One of the most famous exposés was made a number of years ago when a journalist (Wallace, 1958) discovered a man who had been placed and retained in an institution for the mentally retarded for fifty-nine years. He was committed on the basis of prejudicial information as to his social inadequacy. A thorough psychological evaluation, which included an individual intelligence examination, was not provided until after fifty years of institutionalization. This disclosed an I.Q. of 120 and supported the psychologist's impression that the man was normal and should not be incarcerated. Here, obviously, is a compelling illustration of the *proper* use of test scores!

On the other hand, there are many indications of the blatant misuse of test data to incorrectly label and categorize children. Palomares and Johnson (1966) published a report demonstrating that in California Mexican-Americans with significant learning difficulties were ". . . being placed in EMR classes as mentally retarded [and were] incorrectly labeled." Similar findings from other sources have resulted in a number of legal suits in California, one of which resulted in a judicial decree that mandated "a study of home environment, conferences with parents, use of nonverbal as well as verbal tests and placement decision by a broad school committee, *not a single test administration*" (Leary, 1970—emphasis mine). The popular magazines and press seem to be constantly disclosing such cases, which stimulate both public and professional groups to demand reform. Indignation on the part of the black community has steadily increased with accusations that I.Q. tests have "criminal shortcomings" ("San Francisco Schools. . . ," *San Francisco Examiner,* 1970), and with leaders such as Roy Wilkins calling for "tests which relate realistically to ability to perform the required job" (Wilkins, 1971). These stimulants for change have already had a widespread impact on education, as is indicated by a study committee report of the President's Committee on Mental Retardation and the United States Office of Education's Bureau of Education for the Handicapped, calling for a reexamination of "the present system of intelligence testing and classification" ("News and Trends: Environmental Factors. . . ," *Today's Education,* 1970; President's Committee, 1970). In addition to the public outcry, recent happenings within the profession itself have resulted in concerted efforts to deal more effectively with this issue.

RECENT PROFESSIONAL POSITIONS

One of the more recent contributions bearing on the evaluation and development of basic learning abilities is the research findings of Arthur R. Jensen. As psychologists know, Jensen found, as have other investigators, that there is a significant difference in the patterns of abilities among varied ethnic groups. Although he attributed some of the difference to hereditary factors, he emphasized that educators should concern themselves with "teaching basic skills" and "deemphasizing I.Q. tests as a means of assessing gains" (Jensen, 1969, p. 108). With all the controversy involved, it seems that Jensen's call for recognition of what he terms "associative learning abilities" and the use of "learning quotients" has much to offer. In effect, we are recognizing that children and adults vary in learning ability, skill, and style and that different and broader approaches need to be used in evaluation and programming.

These differences are widespread in special education populations; witness my own survey of 743 children placed in classes for the educable mentally retarded. Of these children, 75 percent were from ethnic minorities with distinctive learning styles and difficulties and 59 percent of them fell significantly *above* the classical minus two standard deviations from the mean, a fact sufficient to contradict the label of "mental retardation" (Valett, 1965a). At that time one of my recommendations was for small ungraded classes with specially designed language and experience units; in addition, I called for early recognition of learning disabilities and specific remedial programs. Another early study (Katz, 1964) investigated the effects of desegregation on the performance of black children and concluded with a number of implications for educational practice; one of these was that "track" systems should be abandoned as they tend to freeze teacher's expectations as well as children's self-images; this is now recognized as a forerunner of the Rosenthal experiments cited earlier in this paper. All of these findings, along with many others, emphasize that awareness does exist within the professional establishment itself that changes in both evaluation and educational programming are sorely needed.

More militant demands have now been placed before us. The Association of Black Psychologists is in open warfare against the use of tests which often label black people as uneducable. Williams (1971) has stated that "it is appalling that psychologists have not addressed themselves sufficiently to this abuse of ability testing and subsequent misplacement of Black students." Although the evidence cited both here and in the recent issues of *The School Psychologist Newsletter* would tend to refute this accusation, it does appear justifiable to condemn professional psychological associations for not taking concerted action to bring about the needed changes in psychoeducational practice. Predictably the pressure has continued to increase with one of the most recent actions being a demand for a "moratorium on testing," which was presented to both the California Association of School Psychologists and Psychometrists (CASPP), and the National Association of School Psychologists by a group of minority students in the field of school psychology. This did have an effect and CASPP has now adopted a resolution to condemn reliance on test scores as the sole criterion for the initial placement and classification of any pupil in special classes or programs. CASPP has also called for an immediate moratorium by California school psychologists and psychometrists on such use of test scores for the purpose of placement and classification of children. The Association also endorsed the use and development of "achievement and performance evaluations, tests, and tasks as placement criteria instead of intelligence test scores" (CASPP, 1971).

Concomitantly, legislative action is also being initiated in California to change the system. Following several years of study by the CASPP Supplemental Education and Testing Committees, the Association introduced the "Supplementary Education Act of 1971," which attempts to abolish reliance on single scores and categorical placement for special education purposes. This may be the first time that a professional psychological association has ever taken this kind of legislative action. The Act has now been passed and could drastically change the existing system. In my judgment this would also be a great step forward in coping with the issues under discussion.

However, such a major change in evaluation and programming procedures will demand extended inservice training programs for psychologists on the firing line. If the traditional use of the I.Q. test is to be replaced by a broader evaluation of basic learning abilities, just how is the practitioner to proceed? And most importantly, if the psychologist's emphasis changes from intelligence testing to developmental and remedial programming interventions, qualifying him as a "classroom learning" expert, just how is this possible under existing circumstances?

THE DEVELOPMENTAL TASK APPROACH

At this point in time, I feel that we have encountered some success in this regard and that new and exciting breakthroughs in evaluation and programming lie ahead of us. Let me first comment on what I see as the emerging model that I have termed developmental task analysis.

Esentially, the task analyst is concerned with making a systematic observation of the pupil's behavior in a specific learning situation. His emphasis is on determining *what it is* that the child is to learn and just how well he is doing. He must then decide whether the task expected of the child is an appropriate one considering his total stage of development and the environmental circumstances, such as the classroom or family structure, in which he finds himself. On the basis of his evaluation the task analyst then proceeds to suggest or to design interventions which will enhance the pupil's learning and human development. Most often, these prescriptive interventions require the modification of both the task expectations and the environmental structure with its unique provisions for learning. It is easily recognized that such a model involves more than "I.Q. testing" in that it focuses on the total learning system of which the child is but a part. By definition it also encompasses noncognitive or preintellectual abilities such as motor, sensory, perceptual, and social skills in the psychomotor and affective domains of learning.

Most psychological-test results can be analyzed from a developmental task point of view, and I have devised some profiles for this purpose (Valett, 1965b, 1966a). However, it is most important to recognize that standardized tests are but one part of the developmental task approach—and in my judgment they are of secondary importance. The basic essential data are derived not from standardized-test results, but from systematic observation of actual task performance in the unique learning situation—classroom, home, or job! An approximation of this situation is achieved by selecting work samples or tasks which are very similar to those found in reality and evaluating partial pupil performance accordingly. Many task inventories of basic learning skills and abilities are now available (Slingerland, 1969; Valett, 1966a, 1968, 1969, 1970). These aptly supplement traditional data. In addition, of course, the pupil's performance history and prior learning opportunities must be given careful consideration. By now it should be obvious that although a psychologist or diagnostic-prescriptive teacher may be the coordinator of such an evaluation, he cannot do the job on his own. The pupil, parent, teacher, and specialist must all be cooperatively involved in the evaluation process if subsequent psychoeducational programming is to be meaningful and relevant.

A CASE ILLUSTRATION

An illustration of the primary importance of developmental task analysis can be seen in the case of Billy J., a black boy of low socioeconomic status whose chronological age is nine years one month. Billy was referred for psychoeducational evaluation by a new teacher who described him as being significantly behind in most of his school work, which she felt might be due to "some kind of emotional or neurological problem."

Billy was first examined in the traditional way on the assumption of his school district that an individual intelligence-test score might find him eligible for placement in a "special education class." He was administered the Stanford-Binet L-M and obtained an I.Q. of 84, in consequence of which he was not eligible for special education. The fact that his performance was being compared with a norm group of only one hundred males of comparable age who were all white and upper middle class was not considered; nor was it considered that the Stanford-Binet might not actually be able to provide the essential information necessary to help Billy improve in his school work. So Billy continued in the regular program without change. However, as Billy continued to have learning difficulties, two months later he was referred again. This time he was seen by a different examiner, who decided to administer the Wechsler Intelligence Scale for Children and the Peabody Picture Vocabulary Test. Since the system encouraged only brief reports of test scores, a WISC Performance Scale I.Q. of 89 and a Verbal Scale I.Q. of 77 were recorded—but without reference to the fact that the norm group on this instrument was one hundred white boys. This examiner's report did depart from the usual I.Q. listing, however, in that it noted that he had a "receptive vocabulary" age of seven years four months on the Peabody (the norm group here being 259 cases, white only, from Nashville, Tennessee). Billy was continued in his usual learning situation without any specific recommendations for prescriptive intervention. Within six weeks, he found himself at the bottom of his class, and because his behavior began to change for the worse, his teacher "demanded" some help from psychological services. This time the referral found its way to a new staff member who finally decided that further I.Q. testing would be a hindrance instead of a help. Although he knew that the Illinois Test of Psycholinguistic Abilities was normed on only 25 males at each age group (all white, from Decatur, Illinois), the psychologist decided to use the test in a clinical way; he obtained a total language age of seven years eight months and noted a significantly low auditory-memory performance.

The next step was a decision to become involved with Billy's parents and teacher. The psychologist first interviewed the parents, using the Vineland Social

Maturity Scale (norm group of 25 boys, white only, on the East Coast) and obtained a social age of eight years and six months.

This led him into a discussion of specific parental concerns as indicated by the Developmental Task Analysis. Among several major concerns elaborated by the parents were inability to attend to and complete tasks, throw and catch balls, repeat poems or songs, and imitate words. Several possible strategies now began to appear; they all involved teacher participation. So the psychologist went to the school and systematically observed Billy as he attempted to cope with his assignments. Baseline performance data were accumulated on attending to selected tasks and some word-attack skills. Between them, the teacher and psychologist then administered parts of the Psychoeducational Inventory of Basic Learning Abilities and several subsections of the Slingerland Specific Language Disability Test. Billy's performance was then considered relative to what the teacher and psychologist felt were reasonable expectations for learning. Accordingly, he was judged to have the following learning disabilities:

Motor: Throwing and catching.
Perceptual: Inadequate reaction speed and attending to tasks. Directionality problems in reading and writing. Auditory-memory and sequencing problems.
Language: Word-attack skills (blends). Verbal expression.
Cognitive: Poor classification skills.
Social-Affective: Poor anticipatory responses in group discussion, class projects, and outdoor games. Negative self-concept (failure syndrome).

On the basis of these data no attempt was made to label Billy or to move him to a special class. He was, however, perceived as a boy who was functioning as a slow learner with specific learning disabilities. Cooperatively, a program was planned which included both developmental and remedial education. The parents were involved in some simple home training exercises for selected motor and language skills. Billy moved to a language center which was established in his classroom to provide daily practice exercises in auditory memory and blending. Once a day he attended a reading group in another classroom. A higher-achieving pupil in the same class was assigned to Billy to help him with classification exercises and to play simple games with him (checkers, and the like) requiring planning and anticipatory responses. Billy's teacher acquired two programmed-instruction books for his special use; she also established a deliberate system for encouraging him and rewarding his efforts in an attempt to reverse his negative self-concept. Billy's progress was slow but clearly observable as he began to move forward and achieve meaningful learning objectives. As a result of the cooperative effort of teacher, parents, and psychologist, a plan for learning had been developed which required modification of his home and school environment as well as the designation of his disabilities and priority learning tasks. It is apparent that the traditional approach of I.Q. testing (with reference to nonrepresentative norms) was by itself of questionable help; it was not until a task analysis was made of teacher, parent, and pupil learning criteria and expectations that something meaningful could be done to help Billy learn more effectively. With cooperative involvement in task analysis it could be determined where Billy was in his development, what he should learn next, and some of the ways that could be used to help him make continuous progress toward his learning objectives.

IS IT FEASIBLE?

We must now face the question of feasibility: Is it practical and possible to replace the traditional use of I.Q. testing in the schools with the more functional developmental task analysis? And what has to be done to facilitate such a change, and how can this be put into practice in local school districts?

I believe it is possible to change traditional I.Q. testing in the schools. The models presented by Itard, Piaget, Guilford, and others have already had a significant impact in this regard and will continue to do so in the future. The essential elements needed to further this trend are professional determination and legal sanctions.

The developmental task approach is also practical, much more so than the traditional approach, in its effectiveness in confronting the key issues of what has been learned to date, what needs to be learned next, and what some alternative strategies are for accomplishing these learning goals. It has already compiled a sizable technology for practitioners, hence some of the tools needed are available now for implementation. Also, whereas the traditional approach relegated the basic affective and psychomotor skills as subservient to the cognitive ones, developmental task analysis requires that we look at the entire child including his life style.

The developmental task approach is feasible since it requires a team effort which in essence recognizes the classroom teacher as the key factor in the evaluation and programming of children with learning disabilities. At the same time it insists on broader parental involvement such as is now being evidenced in the use of parents in administering tests (including instruments as sophisticated as the *ITPA*), giving inventories, taking baseline data, and the like, and their subsequent assistance to teachers and psychologists as aides in developmental and remedial training programs. It also brings the pupil himself into the center of the picture by systematically involving him in his own evaluation, goal selection, and self-instruction.

I also believe that a moratorium on the use of test scores alone is a good thing at this stage of our professional development. It will force us as teachers and psychologists alike to use and explore developmental task approaches, and it should have a rapid effect in changing the format of psychoeducational reports to stress learning strengths, weaknesses, and current developmental levels, and to designate specific learning disabilities and prescriptive treatment programs. We will always need and will continue to use standardized tests; but the moratorium will certainly force us to look more carefully at how we use them, and to realize their proper place in the evaluation procedure.

The teacher and school psychologist, being basically pragmatists, also recognize that it is now practical to move with the trend of our time. This trend is definitely toward more humanistic education and toward recognition of and provision for individual differences. The old pigeonholing, categorical, segregated programs must and will be changed accordingly. Such changes will demand modification of our legal provisions and education codes and will also affect the broader social-economic basis of our society which molds the school environment. If broad citizen action groups work together with professional educational and psychological organizations and local parent committees, these changes can be effected for the benefit of the child and all concerned.

Helen Keller once said that we can't have education without revolution. We are now beginning to see a revolution in education which I predict will end in the replacement of the traditional test evaluation with a *pupil-learning-systems* evaluation which emphasizes developmental task analysis, humanistic education, and professional judgments. I hope that we can all continue to work together to that end.

REFERENCES

Binet, Alfred, and Theodore Simon. *The Development of Intelligence in Children.* Translated by E. S. Kite. Vineland, N.J.: The Training School at Vineland, 1916.

Burt, Cyril. "The Inheritance of Mental Ability." *American Psychologist,* Vol. 13, No. 1 (January, 1958).

California Association of School Psychologists and Psychometrists. *Executive Board Minutes,* March 27, 1971, p. 3.

California State Department of Education. *Placement of Underachieving Minority Group Children in Special Classes for the Educable Mentally Retarded. A Report to the California State Legislature as Required by House Resolution 444.* Sacramento, 1970, p. 7.

Dunn, Lloyd M. "Special Education for the Mildly Retarded—Is Much of It Justifiable?" *Exceptional Children,* Vol. 35, No. 1 (September, 1968), pp. 5-22.

Guilford, J. P. *The Nature of Human Intelligence.* New York: McGraw-Hill Book Co., 1967.

Itard, Jean. *The Wild Boy of Aveyron.* New York: Appleton-Century-Crofts, 1962.

Jensen, Arthur R. "How Much Can We Boost I.Q. and Scholastic Achievement? Environment, Heredity and Intelligence." *Harvard Educational Review* Reprint Series No. 2, Cambridge, Mass.: 1969, pp. 1-124.

Katz, I. "Review of Evidence Relating to Effects of Desegregation on the Intellectual Performance of Negroes." *American Psychologist,* Vol. 19 (1964), pp. 381-399.

Leary, Mary Ellen. "Children Who Are Tested in an Alien Environment." *The New Republic Western Edition,* May 30, 1970, p. 18.

McCullers, John C. "G. Stanley Hall's Conception of Mental Development and Some Indications of Its Influence on Developmental Psychology," *American Psychologist,* Vol. 24, No. 12 (December, 1969), p. 110.

McNemar, Quinn. "Lost: Our Intelligence? Why?" *American Psychologist,* Vol. 19, No. 12 (December, 1964), p. 880.

"News and Trends: Environmental Factors Lead to Labeling Children as Retarded." *Today's Education—NEA Journal,* Vol. 59 (1970), p. 3.

Palomares, Uvaldo Hill, and Laverne C. Johnson, "Evaluation of Mexican-American Pupils for EMR Classes," *California Education,* Vol. III, No. 8 (April, 1966), p. 29.

Piaget, Jean. *The Origins of Intelligence in Children.* New York: W. W. Norton and Co., 1952.

President's Committee on Mental Retardation. *The Decisive Decade.* Washington, D.C.: Department of Health, Education, and Welfare, 1970, p. 15.

Rosenthal, Robert, and Lenore Jackson. "Changing Children's I.Q. by Changing Teacher's Expectations." *Professional School Psychology,* Vol. III, edited by Monroe and Gloria Gottsegen. New York: Grune and Stratton, 1969, pp. 172–197.

"San Francisco Schools Act to Halt I.Q. Tests for Blacks." *San Francisco Examiner,* June 17, 1970, p. 4.

Slingerland, Beth. *Screening Test for Identifying Children with Specific Language Disability.* Cambridge, Mass.: Educators Publishing Service, 1969.

Valett, Robert E. "Classification of the Mentally Retarded: An Appraisal," *Psychology in the Schools,* Vol. 2, No. 3 (July, 1965), pp. 210–213.

———. *A Clinical Profile for the Stanford Binet.* Palo Alto, Calif.: Consulting Psychologists Press, 1965.

———. *Developmental Task Analysis.* Belmont, Calif.: Fearon Publishers, 1969.

———. *An Inventory of Primary Skills.* Belmont, Calif.: Fearon Publishers, 1970.

———. *The Psychoeducational Inventory.* Belmont, Calif.: Fearon Publishers, 1968.

———. *A Psychoeducational Profile of Basic Learning Abilities.* Palo Alto, Calif.: Consulting Psychologists Press, 1966.

———. *The Valett Developmental Survey of Basic Learning Abilities,* Palo Alto, Calif.: Consulting Psychologists Press, 1966.

Wallace, Robert. "A Life Time Thrown Away by a Mistake 59 Years Ago," *Life,* Vol. 44 (March 24, 1958), pp. 120–122.

Wilkins, Roy. "Tests: The Black Job Flimflam." *Fresno Bee,* March 28, 1971, 3-D.

Williams, R. "Danger: Testing and Dehumanizing Black Children." *The School Psychologist Newsletter,* Vol. 25 (1971), p. 12.

INDEX

Affective re-education, 87
Alphabet knowledge, 37, 42–45
Alphabet printing, 37, 39
An Inventory of Primary Skills, 37–51, 125–127
Anecdotal record, 8
Anticipatory response, 74
Arithmetic processes, 73
Arithmetic reasoning, 73
Articulation, 71
Associations, 9
Associative learning abilities, 164
Auditory acuity, 67
Auditory awareness, 8
Auditory decoding, 67
Auditory memory, 68
Auditory sequencing, 68
Auditory-vocal association, 68

Balance and rhythm, 65
Baseline data, 96, 133–134, 135, 138
Basic arithmetic, 37, 40
Behavior formula, 7
Body abstraction, 65
Body localization, 65
Body identification, 37, 38
Body-spatial organization, 66
Body-spatial relations, 37, 38
Bohn, Kenneth, 142

California Association of School Psychologists, 165
Class concepts, 37, 46–47
Classification, 73
Classroom environment, 11
Cognitive problem solving, 9

Comprehension, 74
Conceptual-cognitive behavior difficulties, 23
Conceptual skills, 55, 72–74
Consultants, 5, 6
Copying designs, 37, 39
Copying house, 37, 41
Counting, 37, 40
Crawling, 63

Dancing, 64
Descriptive concepts, 37, 50–51
Determining Individual Learning Objectives, 92, 93, 95
Developmental Task Analysis, 31, 117–121, 125, 128–129, 166, 169
Diagnostic-prescriptive process, 4
Diagnostic-prescriptive teaching, 4, 12, 92
Directionality, 66
Dunn, Lloyd, 161

Educational domains, 94
Educational therapy, 149, 155
Effective Teaching, 99
Elliott, Aileen, 103
Environmental determinants, 10
Evaluation summaries, 14
Expressive modalities, 9

Fluency and encoding, 71
Frostig Developmental Test of Visual Perception, 104, 106
General information, 73
General physical health, 65

173

Gililand, Susan, 133
Goal-directed behavior, 90
Goodenough Draw-a-man, 37, 41, 104, 114
Gray Oral Reading Test, 94
Gross motor behavior difficulties, 25
Gross motor development, 55, 63–65
Guidance committee, 5, 142
Guilford, J.P., 63

Hall, G. Stanley, 162
Home training program, 159
Houser, Vernon, 142
Hypotheses, diagnostic, 3

Illinois Test of Psycholinguistic Abilities, 94, 103, 127, 167
Inservice training, 151
Intelligence tests, 161–165
Itard, Jean, 162

Jensen, Arthur, 164
Jumping, 64

Kephart Perceptual-motor Survey, 104, 107
Kourtjian, Harmenia, 114

Language behavior difficulties, 23, 34
Language development, 55, 71–72
Language functioning, 10
Laterality, 67
Learning objectives, 92–100
Learning Resource Center, 147
Learning style, 9
Learning tasks, 15

Mediational processes, 9
Memories, 9

Motor control, 8
Muscular strength, 65
My Goal Record, 90, 91
McDonald Deep Test of Articulation, 133

Number concepts, 72

Paragraph reading, 37, 41
Parent counseling, 149
Parent education, 150
Parent involvement, 5, 13
Peabody Picture Vocabulary Test, 157, 167
Perceptual motor behavior difficulties, 24, 33
Perceptual motor channels, 7
Perceptual motor skills, 55, 67–70
Performance interpretations, 14
Pertinent history, 21
Position in space concepts, 37, 48–49
Prescriptive implications, 57
Prescriptive programs, 6, 15, 97, 110–112, 122–123, 130–132, 136–137, 145–146, 156
Priority learning objectives, 15, 134, 143
Problem description, 20
Psychoeducational Inventory of Basic Learning Abilities
  administration, 54
  materials, 54
  profiles, 56, 58, 59, 60, 75
  task performance ratings, 54
  use, 53–86, 105–109, 117, 124–125, 168
Psychoeducational recommendations, 15
Psychoeducational report, 12
Psychomotor style, 10
Pupil behavior ratings, 22–24
Pupil identification data, 12, 19
Pupil interests, 9

INDEX

175

Pupil involvement, 5
Pupil progress reports, 158
Pupil screening and referral data, 12–13
Pupil self-assessment, 5, 13, 87–91
Pupil strengths and weaknesses, 14
Pupil work sample, 26–28

Reaction speed-dexterity, 66
Reading comprehension, 72
Recommended psychoeducational programs, 58
Reinforcement systems, 98–99, 137, 155
Robinson, Diana, 124
Rolling, 63
Rosenthal, Robert, 161
Running, 64

Self awareness, 90
Self check lists, 87, 89
Self-evaluation questionnaires, 90
Self-identification, 64
Self information, 37, 38
Self Report of Daily Learning Objectives, 98–99
Sensory motor behavior difficulties, 25, 33
Sensory motor integration, 55, 65–67
Sentence copying, 37, 40
Sight vocabulary, 37, 41
Sitting, 63
Skipping, 64
Slingerland Screening Test for Identification of Children with Specific Language Disability, 66
Social acceptance, 74
Social maturity, 74
Social-personal adaptation, 10
Social-personal behavior difficulties, 22, 32
Social skills, 55, 74
Spache Diagnostic Reading Scales, 94

Specific behavior record, 95–96
Spelling, 72
Stanford Achievement Tests, 94
Stanford-Binet, 114, 115, 154, 162, 167
Symbol matching, 37, 40
Tactile discrimination, 8, 66
Task analysis, 142
Target behaviors, 140–141
Taylor-Godwin, H., 142
Teacher objectives, 29
Templin-Darley Test, 133
Teacher expectations, 11
Teacher liaison, 6
The Remediation of Learning Disabilities, 53, 58, 124
Thinking skills, 35–36
Thoughts, 9
Throwing, 64
Time orientation, 67

Value orientations, 9
Value judgments, 74
Vineland Social Maturity Scale, 154, 168
Visual acuity, 8, 68
Visual coordination and pursuit, 68
Visual figure-ground differentiation, 69
Visual form discrimination, 69
Visual memory, 69
Visual motor fine muscle coordination, 70
Visual motor integration, 70
Visual motor memory, 69
Visual motor proficiency, 8
Visual motor spatial form manipulation, 70
Visual motor speed of learning, 70
Vocabulary, 71

Walking, 63
Wechsler Intelligence Scale for

Children, 94, 103, 104, 105, 114, 167
Wide Range Achievement Tests, 94, 104

Word attack skills, 71
Writing, 72
Writing numbers, 37, 39